R

Mrs. Warren's contribution to th[...]
and others in these challenging times commands applause. The copious Biblical content calls forth calm and consolation to the soul. Additionally, the construction and categorization of this work invites the reader to retain this book as a ready reference. It is in my role as a frequent Bible teacher that I will appreciate and utilize this resource to address my students' and my own spiritual needs. I particularly enjoy the "Themes of the Bible" section as an organizing tool to meet those needs. So, I say to the author well done and may God give you the ultimate well done.

— *Mr. Kelson Smith*, *Associate Professor, Dalton State College, Dalton, GA*
Elder & Sabbath School Teacher,
Dalton Seventh-day Adventist Church, Dalton, GA

Writing a book by selecting verses from your daily Bible studies and putting them together in a logical alphabetical format under chosen topics is an innovative idea. This may be a means of reaching people who have only a casual interest in reading the Holy Bible or who may be interested in specific topics only. I am glad that you have been impressed to put your hobby to a wider use. You book has the potential to be a conduit for spreading God's message to many who otherwise may not engage in Bible study.

— *Dr. Leslie Holder*, *Author*

I am impressed with the book especially the categories .This is a creative use of time and a stronghold in life's spiritual battles. I would also like to build a children's program around each category. I really like your creativity as, I too have experienced nights where it's hard to fall asleep. This book would be great to share with friends in need of encouragement. I would enjoy memorizing these texts to strengthen my memory and apply in times of need. Well done and all the best with this project.

— *Marion I A McEachrane*, *BSc, MSc*
Retired Learning Specialist

A lot of hard work was put in the compilation of this book. It will be useful in helping to memorize scriptures and thus keeping God's words in the heart.

— *Eulin Kuranga*, *Retired Healthcare Quality*
Improvement Specialist, Oxford, OH

The material will be of interest and will no doubt appeal and be inspirational to a wide cross-section of individuals as well as groups. For one thing, the organization/presentation is 'fun', not long-winded or complicated. It will be useful & appropriate as a gift for students entering high school and/or newly graduated...planning maybe either to enter the workforce or leaving home for the first time for college overseas.

> — *Emancia Outerbridge*, *Retired Educator and Vestry member of Holy Trinity Anglican Church, Hamilton Parish, Bermuda*

This book is a unique and helpful application of remembering, maintaining, and applying biblical texts and promises through alphabetical recall. Topically arranged, each section is spiritually focused and is an encouraging tool for all believers, and especially those persons seeking guidance in building trust in the Lord Jesus Christ through daily meditation and recitation of His Word.

> — *Eloise L. Symonds*, *Personal Ministries Director and Bible Instructor Bermuda Conference of Seventh-day Adventists*

Just Relax, Recite, and Rest

Scriptural Meditations from A to Zzzz

Marlene Warren

TEACH Services, Inc.
P U B L I S H I N G
www.TEACHServices.com • (800) 367-1844

Copyright © 2021 Marlene Warren
Copyright © 2021 TEACH Services, Inc.
ISBN-13: 978-1-4796-1353-3 (Paperback)
ISBN-13: 978-1-4796-1354-0 (ePub)
Library of Congress Control Number: 2021911017

Published by

TEACH Services, Inc.
P U B L I S H I N G
www.TEACHServices.com • (800) 367-1844

Dedication

This book is lovingly dedicated to the glory of God and to my husband, Cranston, in gratitude for his constant love, encouragement and support.

Author's Notes

- Sometimes only a portion of a verse has been used: the first part is designated as "a" and the second part as "b."
- Nouns and pronouns referring to God have been capitalized throughout.
- *Most* conjunctions at the beginning of verses have been omitted, for example, for, but, so, therefore, etc.
- Differences in spelling of certain words, for example honor/honour, Savior/Saviour are kept as used in a particular version.
- Specifically for letters Q and Z, it was often necessary to select a verse that contained a word beginning with or having that letter within the word; for X, words were chosen that began with "ex."
- Disclaimer: In the instances where a text has been chosen with a key word contained within the text rather than at the beginning, the word has been bolded and written in italics, for example: **K:** God made the beast of the earth according to its ***kind***, cattle according to its ***kind***, and everything that creeps on the earth according to its ***kind***. And God saw that it was good.
- Disclaimer: For visual ease, it was necessary to remove quotation marks that occurred at the beginning of a text and its corresponding closing quotation mark, for example: Come now and let us reason together, says the Lord, "Though your sins are as scarlet, they shall be as white as snow; though they are red like crimson, they shall be like wool."
- In some texts, when the annunciatory clause comes at the beginning of a sentence, it has been omitted when the first word in the quotation begins with the letter being represented. For example, in the section entitled **Isaiah**, the annunciatory clause, "Thus says the Lord," has been omitted in order to use the K at the beginning quotation: Thus says the Lord: "**K**eep justice, and do righteousness…" (Isa. 56:1).

Table of Contents

Introduction

What do you do when you can't fall asleep? Do you toss and turn from side to side for hours? In your mind, do you rehearse all your troubles? Do you think about all the chores for the upcoming day? Do you wonder how you'll ever manage at work the next day? I'm sure these and other physical and mental exercises have been your experience. They have certainly been mine. I never could count sheep!

On one such occasion, in the early morning hours, having tossed about for what seemed like an eternity, I was blessed with a profound thought. Why not try to recite Bible verses in your mind, instead? So began my solution to this dilemma—a recitation of Bible verses from A to Z. Having committed many Bible verses to memory over the years, I was shocked when I reached a certain letter and I couldn't recall a single verse that began with that letter. I lay there saying that letter over and over, and nothing would come to mind.

The next day, I found an empty notepad, labelled the pages from A to Z, and started the process of writing verses that had inspired me over the years.

During my daily Bible study, I would also take note of certain verses and add them to the list. This eventually developed into a spiritual hobby of searching the various books and themes of the Bible for verses to place in alphabetical order. In the process, I have re-read most of the books of the Bible.

"For my thoughts are not your thoughts, neither are your ways my ways," declares the Lord. "As the heavens are higher than the earth, so are my ways higher than your ways and my thoughts than your thoughts" (Isa. 55:8,9, NIV).

The book you hold in your hand is the embodiment of this text. When I embarked on this journey the thought *never* entered my mind that one day I would write this book. In fact, as a retired primary school teacher, my desire has always been to publish a children's picture book based on one of my memoirs. The manuscript was written several years ago, and I have already decided on the title, but God had other thoughts. Maybe later, Marlene, but not right now.

Having amassed numerous slips of paper, sticky notes, notepads, and even a white paper bag, I asked myself, "What do I do with all this?" That's when God downloaded His thoughts, "Write a book!" What could I say? It had already been written. Truly, God is good!

That brings me back to my sleepless nights. You'll be interested to know that falling asleep is seldom an issue for me anymore. Reciting verses in alphabetical order is the first exercise I choose when my head touches the pillow. Very rarely have I made it through the entire alphabet because sleep comes quickly.

I can't claim to have committed all these verses to memory, but I'm finding as I review them from time to time, they more readily come to mind in the night hours. More than that, they are a constant source of inspiration. May God bless you as you embark on this A–Zzzz journey!

Pleasant dreams!

In His service,
Marlene Warren

Themes of the Bible

Creation

All things were made by Him; and without Him was not any thing made that was made.

John 1:3 (KJV)

By the word of the Lord the heavens were made, and all the host of them by the breath of His mouth.

Ps. 33:6

Can you bind the cluster of the Pleiades, or loose the belt of Orion?

Job 38:31

Do you know the ordinances of the heavens? Can you establish their rule on the earth?

Job 38:33 (NRSV)

Everyone who is called by My name, whom I have created for My glory; I have formed him, yes, I have made him.

Isa. 43:7

For He spoke, and it came to be; He commanded, and it stood firm.

Ps. 33:9 (NIV)

God created man in His own image; in the image of God He created him; male and female He created them.

Gen. 1:27

He made the earth by His power; He founded the world by His wisdom and stretched out the heavens by His understanding.

Jer. 51:15 (NIV)

In the beginning God created the heavens and the earth.

Gen. 1:1 (NASB)

J Where were you when I laid the earth's foundation? Tell Me, if you understand.... While the morning stars sang together and all the angels shouted for *joy*?

Job 38:4, 7 (NIV)

K God made the beast of the earth according to its *kind,* cattle according to its *kind*, and everything that creeps on the earth according to its *kind*. And God saw that it was good.

Gen. 1:25

Let them praise the name of the Lord, for at His command they were created.

Ps. 148:5 (NIV)

May you be blessed by the Lord, the Maker of heaven and earth.

Ps. 115:15 (NIV)

Nor was man created for the woman, but woman for the man.

1 Cor. 11:9

On the seventh day God finished the work that He had done, and He rested on the seventh day from all the work that He had done. So God blessed the seventh day and hallowed it, because on it God rested from all the work that He had done in creation.

Gen. 2:2, 3 (NRSV)

P He who is the **Portion** of Jacob is not like these, for He is the Maker of all things, including Israel, the people of His inheritance—the Lord Almighty is His name.

Jer. 10:16 (NIV)

Q Why are your garments hot, when He **quiets** the earth by the south wind? With Him, have you spread out the skies, strong as a cast metal mirror?

Job. 37:17, 18

Rain down, you heavens, from above, and let the skies pour down righteousness; let the earth open, let them bring forth salvation, and let righteousness spring up together. I, the Lord, have created it.

Isa. 45:8

So God created the great creatures of the sea and every living thing with which the water teems and that moves about in it, according to their kinds, and every winged bird according to its kind. And God saw that it was good.

Gen. 1:21 (NIV)

Thus says the Lord, your Redeemer, and He who formed you from the womb: "I am the Lord who makes all things, who stretches out the heavens all alone, who spreads abroad the earth by Myself."

Isa. 44:24

U When He **utters** His voice, there is a multitude of waters in the heavens.

Jer. 10:13a

V He causes the **vapors** to ascend from the ends of the earth. He makes lightning for the rain. He brings the wind out of His treasuries.

Jer. 10:13b

Who has measured the waters in the hollow of His hand and marked off the heavens with a span, enclosed the dust of the earth in a measure, and weighed the mountains in scales and the hills in a balance?

Isa. 40:12 (NRSV)

X The creation waits in eager **expectation** for the children of God to be revealed.

Rom. 8:19 (NIV)

You alone are the Lord; You have made heaven, the heaven of heavens, with all their host, the earth and everything on it, the seas and all that is in them, and You preserve them all. The host of heaven worships You.

Neh. 9:6

Z Let Israel be glad in its Maker; let the children of *Zion* rejoice in their King.

Ps. 149:2 (NRSV)

Don't Worry! Be Happy!

A glad heart makes a cheerful countenance, but by sorrow of the heart the spirit is broken.

Prov. 15:13 (NRSV)

Be glad in the Lord and rejoice, you righteous ones; and shout for joy, all you who are upright in heart.

Ps. 32:11 (NASB)

Consider the lilies, how they grow: they neither toil nor spin; and yet I say to you, even Solomon in all his glory was not arrayed like one of these.

Luke 12:27

Do not worry about tomorrow, for tomorrow will bring worries of its own. Today's trouble is enough for today.

Matt. 6:34 (NRSV)

Enter into His gates with thanksgiving, and into His courts with praise. Be thankful to Him, and bless His name.

Ps. 100:4

For You, Lord, have made me joyful by what You have done, I will sing for joy at the works of Your hands.

Ps. 92:4 (NASB)

Glory in His holy name; let the hearts of those rejoice who seek the Lord!

Ps. 105:3

Happy are those whose help is the God of Jacob, whose hope is in the Lord their God.

Ps. 146:5 (NRSV)

In the multitude of my anxieties within me, your comforts delight my soul.

Ps. 94:19

J These things I have spoken unto you, that My *joy* might remain in you, and that your *joy* may be full.

John 15:11 (KJV)

Know that the Lord has set apart the faithful for Himself; the Lord hears when I call to Him.

Ps. 4:3 (NRSV)

Look at the birds of the air, for they neither sow nor reap nor gather into barns; yet your heavenly Father feeds them. Are you not of more value than they?

Matt. 6:26

Make a joyful noise unto the Lord, all you lands. Serve the Lord with gladness: come before His presence with singing.

Ps. 100:1, 2 (KJV)

Now if God so clothes the grass of the field, which today is, and tomorrow is thrown into the oven, will he not much more clothe you, O you of little faith?

Matt. 6:30

O God, my heart is fixed; I will sing and give praise, even with my glory.

Ps. 108:1 (KJV)

Praise the Lord! For it is good to sing praises to our God; for it is pleasant and praise is beautiful.

Ps. 147:1 (NASB)

Q The Lord your God in your midst, the Mighty One, will save; He will rejoice over you with gladness, He will *quiet* you with His love, He will rejoice over you with singing.

Zeph. 3:17

Rejoice inasmuch as you participate in the sufferings of Christ, so that you may be overjoyed when His glory is revealed.

1 Peter 4:13 (NIV)

Shout joyfully to the Lord, all the earth; be cheerful and sing for joy and sing praises.

Ps. 98:4 (NASB)

Therefore I say to you, do not worry about your life, what you will eat or what you will drink; nor about your body, what you will put on. Is not life more than food and the body more than clothing?

Matt. 6:25

U Blessed are the *undefiled* in the way, who walk in the law of the Lord.

Ps. 119:1 (KJV)

Verily, verily, I say unto you, the servant is not greater than his lord; neither he that is sent greater than he that sent him. If ye know these things, happy are ye if ye do them.

John 13:16, 17 (KJV)

Who of you by worrying can add a single hour to your life? Since you cannot do this very little thing, why do you worry about the rest?

Luke 12:25, 26 (NIV)

X O Lord, You are my God. I will *exalt* You, I will praise Your name, for You have done wonderful things; Your counsels of old are faithfulness and truth.

Isa. 25:1

You will show me the path of life; in Your presence is fullness of joy; at Your right hand are pleasures forevermore.

Ps. 16:11

Zion hears and is glad, and the towns of Judah rejoice, because of Your judgments, O God.

Ps. 97:8 (NRSV)

Eternal Life

And this is eternal life, that they may know You, the only true God, and Jesus Christ whom You have sent.

John 17:3

Blessed be the God and Father of our Lord Jesus Christ, who according to His great mercy has caused us to be born again to a living hope through the resurrection of Jesus Christ from the dead, to obtain an inheritance which is imperishable, undefiled and will not fade away, reserved in heaven for you.

1 Peter 1:3, 4 (NASB)

Charge them that are rich in this world, that they be not highminded, nor to trust in uncertain riches, but in the living God.... That they do good, that they be rich in good works ... laying up in store for themselves a good foundation against the time to come, that they may lay hold on eternal life.

1 Tim. 6:17–19 (KJV)

Do not work for the food that perishes, but for the food that endures for eternal life, which the Son of Man will give you. For it is on Him that God the Father has set His seal.

John 6:27 (NRSV)

Everyone who has left houses or brothers or sisters or father or mother or wife or children or lands, for My name's sake, shall receive a hundredfold, and inherit eternal life.

Matt. 19:29

For the wages of sin is death; but the gift of God is eternal life through Jesus Christ our Lord.

Rom. 6:23 (KJV)

God so loved the world that He gave His only begotten Son, that whoever believes in Him should not perish but have everlasting life.

John 3:16

He who sows to his flesh will of the flesh reap corruption, but he who sows to the Spirit will of the Spirit reap everlasting life.

Gal. 6:8

I consider that the sufferings of this present time are not worthy to be compared with the glory that is to be revealed to us.

Rom. 8:18 (NASB)

Jesus answered and said, "Assuredly, I say to you, there is no one who has left house or brothers or sisters or father or mother or wife or children or lands, for My sake and the gospel's, who shall not receive a hundredfold now in this time...and in the age to come, eternal life."

Mark 10:29, 30

Keep yourselves in the love of God, looking for the mercy of our Lord Jesus Christ unto eternal life.

Jude 1:21

Let what you heard from the beginning abide in you. If what you heard from the beginning abides in you, then you will abide in the Son and in the Father. And this is what He has promised us, eternal life.

1 John 2:24, 25 (NRSV)

My sheep listen to My voice; I know them, and they follow Me. I give them eternal life, and they shall never perish; no one will snatch them out of My hand.

John 10:27, 28 (NIV)

Now they desire a better, that is, a heavenly *country*. Therefore God is not ashamed to be called their God, for He has prepared a city for them.

Heb. 11:16

Our light and momentary troubles are achieving for us an eternal glory that far outweighs them all. So we fix our eyes not on what is seen, but on what is unseen, since what is seen is temporary, but what is unseen is eternal.

2 Cor. 4:17, 18 (NIV)

Paul and Barnabas answered them boldly: "We had to speak the word of God to you first. Since you reject it and do not consider yourselves worthy of eternal life, we now turn to the Gentiles."

Acts 13:46 (NIV)

Q The Lord your God in your midst, the Mighty One, will save; He will rejoice over you with gladness, He will *quiet you* with His love, He will rejoice over you with singing.

Zeph. 3:17

Riches do not benefit on the day of wrath, but righteousness rescues from death.

Prov. 11:4 (NASB)

So He said to him, "Why do you call Me good? No one is good but One, that is, God. But if you want to enter into life, keep the commandments."

Matt. 19:17

These things I have written to you who believe in the name of the Son of God, so that you may know that you have eternal life.

1 John 5:13 (NASB)

Unless you are converted and become as little children, you will by no means enter the kingdom of heaven.

Matt. 18:3

Verily, verily, I say unto you, He that heareth my word, and believeth on him that sent me, hath everlasting life, and shall not come into condemnation; but is passed from death unto life.

John 5:24 (KJV)

When the Gentiles heard this, they were glad and praised the word of the Lord; and as many as had been destined for eternal life became believers.

Acts 13:48 (NRSV)

X For thus says the Lord: "Behold, I will *extend* peace to her like a river, and the glory of the Gentiles like a flowing stream. Then you shall feed; on *her* sides shall you be carried, and be dandled on *her* knees."

Isa. 66:12

You search the Scriptures, for in them you think you have eternal life; and these are they which testify of Me.

John 5:39

Z Then you will know that I am the Lord your God, dwelling in **Zion**, My holy mountain. So Jerusalem will be holy, and strangers will no longer pass through it.

Joel 3:17 (NASB)

Faith

As the body without the spirit is dead so faith without works is dead also.
James 2:26 (KJV)

By faith Abraham, when put to the test, offered up Isaac. He who had received the promises was ready to offer up his only son.
Heb. 11:17 (NRSV)

Christ has redeemed us from the curse of the law, having become a curse for us... that the blessing of Abraham might come upon the Gentiles in Christ Jesus, that we might receive the promise of the Spirit through faith.
Gal. 3:13, 14

Do you see that faith was working together with his works, and by works, faith was made perfect?
James 2:22

Esteeming the reproach of Christ greater riches than the treasures in Egypt: for he had respect unto the recompence of the reward. By faith he forsook Egypt, not fearing the wrath of the king: for he endured, as seeing Him who is invisible.

Heb. 11:26, 27 (KJV)

Faith comes from hearing, and hearing by the word of Christ.

Rom. 10:17 (NASB)

Guard what has been entrusted to your care. Turn away from godless chatter and the opposing ideas of what is falsely called knowledge, which some have professed and in doing so have departed from the faith.

1 Tim. 6:20, 21 (NIV)

Having been justified by faith, we have peace with God through our Lord Jesus Christ.

Rom. 5:1 (NASB)

I have fought the good fight, I have finished the race, I have kept the faith.

2 Tim. 4:7

Jesus said to them, ... "I say to you, if you have faith as a mustard seed, you will say to this mountain, 'Move from here to there,' and it will move; and nothing will be impossible for you."

Matt. 17:20

Know that only those who are of faith are sons of Abraham.

Gal. 3:7

Looking unto Jesus, the author and finisher of our faith, who for the joy that was set before Him endured the cross, despising the shame, and has sat down at the right hand of the throne of God.

Heb. 12:2

My brethren, have not the faith of our Lord Jesus Christ, the Lord of glory, with respect of persons.

James 2:1 (KJV)

Now faith is the substance of things hoped for, the evidence of things not seen.

Heb. 11:1

Only conduct yourselves in a manner worthy of the gospel of Christ, so that whether I come and see you or remain absent, I will hear of you that you are standing firm in one spirit, with one mind striving together for the faith of the gospel.

Phil. 1:27 (NASB)

P The *prayer* offered in faith will restore the one who is sick, and the Lord will raise him up, and if he has committed sins, they will be forgiven him.

James 5:15 (NASB)

Q Who through faith subdued kingdoms, wrought righteousness, obtained promises, stopped the mouths of lions. *Quenched* the violence of fire, escaped the edge of the sword, out of weakness were made strong, waxed valiant in fight, turned to flight the armies of the aliens.

Heb. 11:33, 34 (KJV)

Remember your leaders, those who spoke the word of God to you; consider the outcome of their way of life, and imitate their faith.

Heb. 13:7 (NRSV)

Someone will say, "You have faith, and I have works." Show me your faith without your works, and I will show you my faith by my works.

James 2:18

Those who rely on faith are blessed along with Abraham, the man of faith.

Gal. 3:9 (NIV)

U By faith we *understand* that the worlds were prepared by the word of God, so that what is seen was made from things that are not visible.

Heb. 11:3 (NRSV)

V If those who are of the Law are heirs, faith is made *void* and the promise is nullified.

Rom. 4:14 (NASB)

Without faith it is impossible to please Him, for he who comes to God must believe that He is, and that He is a rewarder of those who diligently seek Him.

Heb. 11:6

X By faith Abel offered to God a more *excellent* sacrifice than Cain, through which he obtained witness that he was righteous, God testifying of his gifts; and through it he being dead still speaks.

Heb. 11:4

You all are sons and daughters of God through faith in Christ Jesus.

Gal. 3:26 (NASB)

Z Behold, I lay in *Zion* a chief cornerstone, elect, precious, and he who believes on Him will by no means be put to shame.

1 Peter 2:6

Grace

As sin reigned in death, so also grace would reign through righteousness to eternal life through Jesus Christ our Lord.

Rom. 5:21 (NASB)

By grace you have been saved through faith; and this is not of yourselves, it is the gift of God; not a result of works, so that no one may boast.

Eph. 2:8, 9 (NASB)

C The *Child* grew and became strong in spirit, filled with wisdom; and the grace of God was upon Him.

Luke 2:40

Do not be carried away by all kinds of strange teachings. It is good for our hearts to be strengthened by grace, not by eating ceremonial foods, which is of no benefit to those who do so.

Heb. 13:9 (NIV)

Even so then at this present time also there is a remnant according to the election of grace.

Rom. 11:5 (KJV)

For the grace of God has appeared, bringing salvation to all, training us to renounce impiety and worldly passions, and in the present age to live lives that are self-controlled, upright, and godly.

Titus 2:11, 12 (NRSV)

God is able to make all grace overflow to you, so that, always having all sufficiency in everything, you may have an abundance for every good deed.

2 Cor. 9:8 (NASB)

Having been justified by His grace, we might become heirs according to the hope of eternal life.

Titus 3:7 (NRSV)

If by the one man's offense death reigned through the one, much more those who receive abundance of grace and of the gift of righteousness will reign in life through the One, Jesus Christ.

Rom. 5:17

Just as He chose us in Him before the foundation of the world, that we would be holy and blameless before Him…to the praise of the glory of His grace, which He favored us in the Beloved.

Eph. 1:4, 6 (NASB)

Keep sound wisdom and discretion; so they will be life to your soul and grace to your neck.

Prov. 3:21b, 22

Let us therefore come boldly unto the throne of grace, that we may obtain mercy, and find grace to help in time of need.

Heb. 4:16 (KJV)

May the God of all grace, who called us to His eternal glory by Christ Jesus, after you have suffered a while, perfect, establish, strengthen, and settle you.

1 Peter 5:10

Noah found grace in the eyes of the Lord.

Gen. 6:8

On the contrary, I worked harder than any of them—though it was not I, but the grace of God that is with me.

1 Cor. 15:10b (NRSV)

Pursue peace with all people, and holiness, without which no one will see the Lord: looking carefully lest anyone fall short of the grace of God.

Heb. 12:14, 15a

Q The Lord is merciful and gracious…. He has not dealt with us according to our sins, nor punished us according to our *iniquities.*

Ps. 103:8a, 10

Remember my chains. Grace be with you. Amen.

Col. 4:18b

Sin shall not be master over you, for you are not under the Law but under grace.

Rom. 6:14 (NASB)

To me, who am less than the least of all the saints, this grace was given, that I should preach among the Gentiles the unsearchable riches of Christ.

Eph. 3:8

U For the Lord God is a sun and shield: the Lord will give grace and glory: no good thing will He withhold from them that walk *uprightly.*

Ps. 84:11 (KJV)

V The king loved Esther more than all the *other* women, and she obtained grace and favor in his sight more than all the *virgins*; so he set the royal crown upon her head and made her queen instead of *Vashti.*

Esther 2:17

We do see Jesus, who for a little while was made lower than the angels, now crowned with glory and honor because of the suffering of death, so that by the grace of God He might taste death for everyone.

Heb. 2:9 (NRSV)

X [God] raised us up together, and made us sit together in the heavenly places in Christ Jesus, that in the ages to come He might show the *exceeding* riches of His grace in His kindness toward us in Christ Jesus.

Eph. 2:6, 7

You therefore, my son, be strong in the grace that is in Christ Jesus.

2 Tim. 2:1 (NASB)

Z He answered and said to me: "This is the word of the Lord to *Zerubbabel:* 'Not by might nor by power, but by My Spirit,' says the Lord of hosts. 'Who are you, O great mountain? Before *Zerubbabel* you shall become a plain! And he shall bring forth the capstone with shouts of "Grace, grace to it!"

Zech. 4:6, 7

Hope

As for me, I will always have hope; I will praise You more and more.

Ps. 71:14 (NIV)

Blessed be the God and Father of our Lord Jesus Christ, who according to His great mercy has caused us to be born again to a living hope through the resurrection of Jesus Christ from the dead.

1 Peter 1:3 (NASB)

Chasten your son while there is hope, and do not set your heart on his destruction.

Prov. 19:18

Do you see a person who is hasty in his words? There is more hope for a fool than for him.

Prov. 29:20 (NASB)

Everyone who has this hope in Him purifies himself, just as He is pure.

1 John 3:3

Faith is the assurance of things hoped for, the conviction of things not seen.

Heb. 11:1 (NRSV)

Gird up the loins of your mind, be sober, and rest your hope fully upon the grace that is to be brought to you at the revelation of Jesus Christ.

1 Peter 1:13

Having been justified by faith, we have peace with God through our Lord Jesus Christ, through whom also we have access by faith into this grace in which we stand, and rejoice in hope of the glory of God.

Rom. 5:1, 2

I know the plans I have for you, declares the Lord, plans to prosper you and not to harm you, plans to give you hope and a future.

Jer. 29:11 (NIV)

J That being *justified* by His grace, we should be made heirs according to the hope of eternal life.

Titus 3:7 (KJV)

K To them God chose to make **known** how great among the Gentiles are the riches of the glory of this mystery, which is Christ in you, the hope of glory.

Col. 1:27 (NRSV)

Let us who are of the day be sober, putting on the breastplate of faith and love, and as a helmet the hope of salvation.

1 Thess. 5:8

May the God of hope fill you with all joy and peace as you trust in Him, so that you may overflow with hope by the power of the Holy Spirit.

Rom. 15:13 (NIV)

Now hope does not disappoint, because the love of God has been poured out in our hearts by the Holy Spirit who was given to us.

Rom. 5:5

O Israel, hope in the Lord! For with the Lord there is steadfast love, and with Him is great power to redeem.

Ps. 130:7 (NRSV)

Paul, a servant of God and an apostle of Jesus Christ to further the faith of God's elect and their knowledge of the truth that leads to godliness—in the hope of eternal life, which God, who does not lie, promised before the beginning of time.

Titus 1:1, 2 (NIV)

Q Now when Herod saw Jesus, he was exceedingly glad…and he hoped to see some miracle done by Him. Then he **questioned** Him with many words, but He answered him nothing.

Luke 23:8, 9

Remember Your word to Your servant, in which You have made me hope.

Ps. 119:49 (NRSV)

Sanctify Christ as Lord in your hearts, always being ready to make a defense to everyone who asks you to give an account for the hope that is in you, yet with gentleness and respect.

1 Peter 3:15 (NASB)

This hope we have as an anchor of the soul, both sure and steadfast, and which enters the Presence behind the veil.

Heb. 6:19

U Take not the word of truth *utterly* out of my mouth, for I have hoped in Your ordinances.

Ps. 119:43

V Truly in *vain* is salvation hoped for from the hills, and from the multitude of mountains: truly in the Lord our God is the salvation of Israel.

Jer. 3:23 (KJV)

We were saved in this hope, but hope that is seen is not hope; for why does one still hope for what he sees?

Rom. 8:24

X It is my eager *expectation* and hope that I will not be put to shame in any way, but that by my speaking with all boldness, Christ will be *exalted* now as always in my body, whether by life or by death.

Phil. 1:20 (NRSV)

You are my hope, O Lord God; You are my trust from my youth.

Ps. 71:5

Z The Lord also shall roar out of *Zion*, and utter His voice from Jerusalem; and the heavens and the earth shall shake: but the Lord will be the hope of His people, and the strength of the children of Israel.

Joel 3:16 (KJV)

Love

Above all things have fervent love for one another, for "love will cover a multitude of sins."

1 Peter 4:8

Beloved, if God so loved us, we also ought to love one another.

1 John 4:11 (NASB)

Concerning brotherly love, you have no need that I should write to you, for you yourselves are taught by God to love one another.

1 Thess. 4:9

Do not love the world nor the things in the world. If anyone loves the world, the love of the Father is not in him.

1 John 2:15 (NASB)

Eye has not seen, nor ear heard, nor have entered into the heart of man the things which God has prepared for those who love Him.

1 Cor. 2:9

For God so loved the world that He gave His only begotten Son, that whoever believes in Him should not perish but have everlasting life.

John 3:16

Greater love has no one than this: to lay down one's life for one's friends.

John 15:13 (NIV)

He who loves his brother abides in the light, and there is no cause for stumbling in him.

1 John 2:10

If someone says, "I love God," and yet he hates his brother or sister, he is a liar; for the one who does not love his brother and sister whom he has seen, cannot love God, whom he has not seen.

1 John 4:20 (NASB)

Jesus answered and said to him, "If anyone loves Me, he will follow My word; and My Father will love him, and We will come to him and make Our dwelling with him."

John 14:23 (NASB)

Keep yourselves in the love of God; look forward to the mercy of our Lord Jesus Christ that leads to eternal life.

Jude 1:21 (NRSV)

Love is patient, love is kind, it is not jealous; love does not brag, it is not arrogant.

1 Cor. 13:4 (NASB)

My little children, let us not love in word, neither in tongue; but in deed and in truth.

1 John 3:18 (KJV)

Nevertheless let each one of you in particular so love his own wife as himself, and let the wife see that she respects her husband.

Eph. 5:33

Owe nothing to anyone except to love one another; for the one who loves his neighbor has fulfilled the law.

Rom. 13:8 (NASB)

Perfect love casts out fear, because fear involves torment. But he who fears has not been made perfect in love.

1 John 4:18b

Q Many waters cannot **quench** love, nor can the floods drown it. If a man would give for love all the wealth of his house, it would be utterly despised.

Song of Sol. 8:7

Revive me, O Lord, according to Your lovingkindness.

Ps. 119:159b

Set me as a seal upon your heart, as a seal upon your arm; for love is strong as death, passion fierce as the grave.

Song of Sol. 8:6a (NRSV)

This is My commandment, that you love one another, just as I have loved you.

John 15:12 (NASB)

U How precious is Your lovingkindness, O God! Therefore the children of men put their trust **unde**r the shadow of Your wings.

Ps. 36:7

V A **voice**! My beloved was knocking: 'Open to me, my sister, my darling, my dove, my perfect one! For my head is drenched with dew, my locks with the damp of the night.

Song of Sol. 5:2b (NASB)

We love Him because He first loved us.

1 John 4:19

X Let no one look down on your youthfulness, but rather in speech, conduct, love, faith, and purity, show yourself an **example** of those who believe.

1 Tim. 4:12 (NASB)

You shall love the Lord your God with all your heart, with all your soul, and with all your strength.

Deut. 6:5

Z Do not be afraid *Zion*…. The Lord your God is in your midst, a victorious warrior. He will rejoice over you with joy, He will be quiet in His love, He will rejoice over you with shouts of joy.

Zeph. 3:16, 17 (NASB)

Mercy

Although I was formerly a blasphemer, a persecutor, and an insolent man; but I obtained mercy because I did it ignorantly in unbelief.

1 Tim. 1:13

Blessed are the merciful: for they shall obtain mercy.

Matt. 5:7 (KJV)

Come now, and let us debate your case," says the Lord, "Though your sins are as scarlet, they shall become as white as snow; though they are red like crimson, they will be like wool."

Isa. 1:18 (NASB)

Do not withhold Your tender mercies from me, O Lord; let Your loving kindness and Your truth continually preserve me.

Ps. 40:11

E The *earth,* O Lord, is full of Your mercy; teach me Your statutes.

Ps. 119:64

For I have said, "Mercy shall be built up forever; Your faithfulness You shall establish in the very heavens."

Ps. 89:2

Go and learn what this means: 'I desire mercy and not sacrifice.' For I did not come to call the righteous, but sinners, to repentance.

Matt. 9:13

He has shown you, O mortal, what is good. And what does the Lord require of you? To act justly and to love mercy and to walk humbly with your God.

Mic. 6:8 (NIV)

I will sing of the mercies of the Lord forever; with my mouth will I make known Your faithfulness to all generations.

Ps. 89:1

Judgment will be merciless to one who has shown no mercy; mercy triumphs over judgment.

James 2:13 (NASB)

Keeping mercy for thousands, forgiving iniquity and transgression and sin, and that will by no means clear the guilty.

Exod. 34:7 (KJV)

Let not mercy and truth forsake you; bind them around your neck, write them on the tablet of your heart.

Prov. 3:3

Mercy and truth are met together; righteousness and peace have kissed each other.

Ps. 85:10 (KJV)

Not by works of righteousness which we have done, but according to His mercy He saved us, by the washing of regeneration and renewing of the Holy Ghost.

Titus 3:5 (KJV)

Oh, give thanks to the Lord, for He is good! For His mercy endures forever.

1 Chron. 16:34

Pardon the iniquity of this people, I pray, according to the greatness of Your mercy, just as You have forgiven this people, from Egypt even until now.

Num. 14:19

Q The Lord is longsuffering and abundant in mercy, forgiving *iniquity* and transgression; but He by no means clears the guilty, visiting the *iniquity* of the fathers on the children to the third and fourth generation.

Num. 14:18

Righteousness and justice are the foundation of Your throne; mercy and truth go before Your face.

Ps. 89:14

Show us Your mercy, Lord, and grant us Your salvation.

Ps. 85:7

To the Lord our God belong mercy and forgiveness, for we have rebelled against Him.

Dan. 9:9 (NRSV)

U Behold, as the eyes of servants look *unto* the hand of their masters, and as the eyes of a maiden *unto* the hand of her mistress; so our eyes wait *upon* the Lord our God, *until* that He have mercy *upon* us.

Ps. 123:2 (KJV)

V Now concerning *virgins*, I have no command of the Lord, but I am offering direction as one who by the mercy of the Lord is trustworthy.

1 Cor. 7:25 (NASB)

Who is a God like You, who pardons sin and forgives the transgression of the remnant of His inheritance? You do not stay angry forever but delight to show mercy.

Mic. 7:18 (NIV)

X His mercy is to generation after generation toward those who fear Him. He has done mighty deeds with His arm; He has scattered those who were proud in the thoughts of their hearts. He has put down rulers from their thrones, and has *exalted* those who were humble.

Luke 1:50 –52 (NASB)

Your mercy is great above the heavens, and Your truth reaches to the clouds.

Ps. 108:4

Z Return, faithless Israel, says the Lord. I will not look on you in anger, for I am merciful, says the Lord.... I will take you, one from a city and two from a family, and I will bring you to *Zion*.

Jer. 3:12, 14b (NRSV)

Peace

All your children shall be taught by the Lord, and great shall be the peace of your children.

Isa. 54:13

Blessed are the peacemakers: for they shall be called the children of God.

Matt. 5:9 (KJV)

Creating the praise of the lips. Peace, peace to him who is far and to him who is near," says the Lord, "and I will heal him."

Isa. 57:19 (NASB)

Depart from evil, and do good; seek peace, and pursue it.

Ps. 34:14 (KJV)

Even a fool is counted wise when he holds his peace; when he shuts his lips, he is considered perceptive.

Prov. 17:28

For the mountains may depart and the hills be removed, but My steadfast love shall not depart from you, and My covenant of peace shall not be removed, says the Lord, who has compassion on you.

Isa. 54:10 (NRSV)

Great peace have those who love Your law; nothing can make them stumble.

Ps. 119:165 (NRSV)

Having been justified by faith, we have peace with God through our Lord Jesus Christ.

Rom. 5:1

I will both lie down in peace, and sleep; for You alone, O Lord, make me dwell in safety.

Ps. 4:8

J There is no *justice* in their ways; they have made themselves crooked paths; whoever takes that way shall not know peace.

Isa. 59:8b

K Endeavour(ing) to *keep* the unity of the Spirit in the bond of peace.

Eph. 4:3 (KJV)

Let the peace of Christ rule in your hearts, to which indeed you were called in the one body. And be thankful.

Col. 3:15 (NRSV)

My people will abide in a peaceful habitation, in secure dwellings, and in quiet resting places.

Isa. 32:18 (NRSV)

Now the fruit of righteousness is sown in peace by those who make peace.

James 3:18

Oh, that you had heeded My commandments! Then your peace would have been like a river, and your righteousness like the waves of the sea.

Isa. 48:18

Peace I leave you, My peace I give to you; not as the world gives, do I give to you. Do not let your heart be troubled, nor fearful.

John 14:27 (NASB)

Q I exhort therefore, that, first of all, supplications, prayers, intercessions, and giving of thanks, be made for all men; for kings, and for all that are in authority; that we may lead a *quiet* and peaceable life in all godliness and honesty.

1 Tim. 2:1, 2 (KJV)

R Then He arose, and *rebuked* the wind, and said to the sea, "Peace, be still!" And the wind ceased and there was a great calm.

Mark 4:39

Suddenly there was with the angel a multitude of the heavenly host praising God, and saying, Glory to God in the highest, and on earth peace,
good will toward men.

                                                        Luke 2:13, 14 (KJV)

These things I have spoken to you so that in Me you may have peace. In
the world you have tribulation, but take courage; I have overcome the
world.

                                                           John 16:33 (NASB)

Unto us a Child is born, unto us a Son is given; and the government shall
be upon His shoulder. And His name will be called Wonderful, Counselor,
Mighty God, Everlasting Father, Prince of Peace.

                                                                   Isa. 9:6

Violence will not be heard again in your land, nor devastation or destruction within your borders; but you will call your walls salvation, and your
gates praise.

                                                          Isa. 60:18 (NASB)

When a person's ways are pleasing to the Lord, He causes even his enemies to make peace with him.

                                                          Prov. 16:7 (NASB)

X Thus says the Lord: "Behold, I will *extend* peace to her like a river, and
the glory of the Gentiles like a flowing stream.

                                                                Isa. 66:12a

You will keep him in perfect peace, whose mind is stayed on You, because
he trusts in You.

                                                                  Isa. 26:3

Z How beautiful on the mountains are the feet of those who bring good
news, who proclaim peace, who bring good tidings, who proclaim salvation, who say to *Zion*, "Your God reigns!"

                                                            Isa. 52:7 (NIV)

Praise

All the earth will worship You, and will sing praises to You; they will sing praises to Your name.

Ps. 66:4 (NASB)

B From *birth* I have relied on You; You *brought* me forth from my mother's womb. I will ever praise You.

Ps. 71:6 (NIV)

Certainly God has heard me; He has attended to the voice of my prayer. Blessed be God, who has not turned away my prayer, nor His mercy from me!

Ps. 66:19, 20

Do You hear what these are saying? And Jesus said to them, "Yes. Have you never read, 'Out of the mouth of babes and nursing infants You have perfected praise?'"

Matt. 21:16b

Every day I will bless You, and I will praise Your name forever and ever.

Ps. 145:2 (NASB)

From the rising of the sun to its setting, the name of the Lord is to be praised.

Ps. 113:3 (NASB)

Great is the Lord, and greatly to be praised; His greatness is unsearchable.

Ps. 145:3 (NRSV)

He is your glory and He is your God, who has done these great and awesome things for you which your eyes have seen.

Deut. 10:21 (NASB)

Judge nothing before the time, until the Lord comes, who will both bring to light the hidden things of darkness and reveal the counsels of the hearts. Then each one's praise will come from God.

1 Cor. 4:5

Kings of the earth, and all people; princes, and all judges of the earth: Both young men, and maidens; old men, and children. Let them praise the name of the Lord: for His name alone is excellent; His glory is above the earth and heaven.

Ps. 148:11–13 (KJV)

Let everything that has breath praise the Lord. Praise the Lord!

Ps. 150:6

My mouth will speak the praise of the Lord, and all flesh will bless His holy name forever and ever.

Ps. 145:21 (NASB)

Now I, Nebuchadnezzar, praise, exalt, and honor the King of heaven, for all His works are true and His ways just; and He is able to humble those who walk in pride.

Dan. 4:37 (NASB)

Open to me the gates of righteousness; I will go through them, and I will praise the Lord.

Ps. 118:19

Praise the Lord! For it is good to sing praises to our God; for it is pleasant and praise is beautiful.

Ps. 147:1 (NASB)

Q They surrounded me like bees; they were *quenched* like a fire of thorns; for in the name of the Lord I will destroy them. You pushed me violently, that I might fall, but the Lord helped me. The Lord is my strength and song, and He has become my salvation.

Ps. 118:12–14

Rejoice in the Lord, O you righteous! For praise from the upright is beautiful.

Ps. 33:1

Suddenly there was with the angel a multitude of the heavenly host praising God, and saying, Glory to God in the highest, and on earth peace, goodwill toward men!

Luke 2:13, 14 (KJV)

The waters covered their enemies; there was not one of them left. Then they believed in His words; they sang His praise.

Ps. 106:11, 12

U Who can *utter* the mighty acts of the Lord? Who can declare all His praise?

Ps. 106:2

Violence shall no more be heard in your land, devastation or destruction within your borders; you shall call your walls Salvation, and your gates Praise.

Isa. 60:18 (NRSV)

While I live will I praise the Lord: I will sing praises unto my God while I have any being.

Ps. 146:2 (KJV)

X He has *exalted* the horn of His people, the praise of all His saints—of the people of Israel, a people near to Him. Praise the Lord!

Ps. 148:14

You are a chosen generation, a royal priesthood, a holy nation, His own special people, that you may proclaim the praises of Him who called you out of darkness into His marvelous light.

1 Peter 2:9

Z Praise the Lord. Sing to the Lord a new song, His praise in the assembly of His faithful people. Let Israel rejoice in their Maker; let the people of *Zion* be glad in their King.

Ps. 149:1, 2 (NIV)

Prayer

As for me, I trust in You, O Lord; I say, "You are my God."

Ps. 31:14

Be careful for nothing; but in every thing by prayer and supplication with thanksgiving let your requests be made known unto God.

Phil. 4:6 (KJV)

Create in me a clean heart, O God; and renew a right spirit within me.

Ps. 51:10 (KJV)

Direct my steps by Your word, and let no iniquity have dominion over me.

Ps. 119:133

Examine me, O Lord, and put me to the test; refine my mind and my heart.

Ps. 26:2 (NASB)

Forgive us our debts, as we forgive our debtors.

Matt. 6:12

Give heed to the voice of my cry, my King and my God, for to You I will pray.

Ps. 5:2

Hear from heaven, from Your dwelling place, their prayer and pleadings, and maintain their cause, and forgive Your people who have sinned against You.

2 Chron. 6:39 (NASB)

I will both lie down and sleep in peace; for You alone, O Lord, make me lie down in safety.

Ps. 4:8 (NRSV)

Jesus spoke these words, lifted His eyes to heaven, and said: "Father, the hour has come. Glorify Your Son, that Your Son also may glorify You."

John 17:1

Keep me as the apple of Your eye; hide me under the shadow of Your wings.

> Ps. 17:8

Let us therefore come boldly unto the throne of grace, that we may obtain mercy, and find grace to help in time of need.

> Heb. 4:16 (KJV)

Make Your face to shine upon Your servant; save me in Your faithfulness.

> Ps. 31:16 (NASB)

Now Jabez was more honorable than his brothers...and Jabez called on the God of Israel saying, "Oh, that You would bless me indeed and enlarge my territory, that Your hand would be with me, and that You would keep me from evil, that I may not cause pain!" So God granted him what he requested.

> 1 Chron. 4:9a, 10

Our Father, who is in heaven, hallowed be Your name. Your kingdom come. Your will be done, on earth as it is in heaven.

> Matt. 6:9b, 10 (NASB)

Purge me with hyssop, and I shall be clean; wash me, and I shall be whiter than snow.

> Ps. 51:7

Q Then the people cried out to Moses, and when Moses prayed to the Lord, the fire was *quenched.*

> Num. 11:2

Revive me according to Your faithfulness, so that I may keep the testimony of Your mouth.

> Ps. 119:88 (NASB)

Search me, O God, and know my heart; try me, and know my thoughts.
> Ps. 139:23 (KJV)

Teach me Your way, O Lord, and lead me in a smooth path, because of my enemies.

Ps. 27:11

Unite my heart to fear Your name. I will praise You, O Lord my God, with all my heart, and I will glorify Your name forevermore.

Ps. 86:11b, 12

V Then she [Hannah] made a *vow* and said, "O Lord of hosts, if You will indeed look on the affliction of Your maidservant and remember me, and not forget Your maidservant, but will give Your maidservant a male child, then I will give him to the Lord all the days of his life, and no razor shall come upon his head."

1 Sam. 1:11

Watch and pray so that you will not fall into temptation. The spirit is willing, but the flesh is weak.

Matt. 26:41 (NIV)

X Be *exalted* above the heavens, God, and may Your glory be above all the earth.

Ps. 108:5 (NASB)

You have heard that it was said, 'You shall love your neighbor and hate your enemy.' But I say to you, love your enemies, bless those who curse you, do good to those who hate you, and pray for those who despitefully use you and persecute you.

Matt. 5:43, 44

Z Let all those who hate *Zion* be put to shame and turned back.

Ps. 129:5

Promises

As one whom his mother comforts, so I will comfort you; and you shall be comforted in Jerusalem.

Isa. 66:13

Behold, I stand at the door and knock; if anyone hears My voice and opens the door, I will come in to him and will dine with him, and he with Me.

Rev. 3:20 (NASB)

Call to Me, and I will answer you, and show you great and mighty things, which you do not know.

Jer. 33:3

Did I not tell you that if you believe, you will see the glory of God?

John 11:40 (NIV)

Even to your old age I am He, even when you turn gray I will carry you. I have made, and I will bear; I will carry and will save.

Isa. 46:4 (NRSV)

For I am the Lord your God who takes hold of your right hand and says to you, Do not fear; I will help you.

Isa. 41:13 (NIV)

Gentiles shall come to your light, and kings to the brightness of your rising.

Isa. 60:3

Have I not commanded you? Be strong and courageous. Do not be afraid; do not be discouraged, for the Lord your God will be with you wherever you go.

Josh. 1:9 (NIV)

If you abide in Me, and My words abide in you, ask for whatever you wish, and it will be done for you.

John 15:7 (NRSV)

Jesus said to her, "I am the resurrection and the life. He who believes in Me, though he may die, he shall live."

John 11:25

Keep justice, and do righteousness, for My salvation is about to come, and My righteousness to be revealed.

Isa. 56:1b

Let the wicked forsake his way, and the unrighteous man his thoughts: and let him return unto the Lord, and He will have mercy on him; and to our God, for He will abundantly pardon.

Isa. 55:7 (KJV)

My sheep listen to My voice, and I know them, and they follow Me; and I give them eternal life, and they will never perish; and no one will snatch them out of My hand.

John 10:27, 28 (NASB)

No weapon formed against you shall prosper, and every tongue which rises against you in judgment you shall condemn.

Isa. 54:17a

Other sheep I have, which are not of this fold: them also I must bring, and they shall hear My voice; and there will be one fold, and one Shepherd.

John 10:16 (KJV)

Peace I leave with you, My peace I give to you; not as the world gives do I give to you. Let not your heart be troubled, neither let it be afraid.

John 14:27

Q The Lord your God in your midst, the Mighty One, will save; He will rejoice over you with gladness, He will *quiet* you with His love, He will rejoice over you with singing.

Zeph. 3:17

Return to Me, says the Lord of hosts, and I will return to you, says the Lord of hosts.

Zech. 1:3b (NRSV)

Seek first the kingdom of God and His righteousness, and all these things shall be added to you.

Matt. 6:33

Take My yoke upon you and learn from Me, for I am gentle and humble in heart, and you will find rest for your souls.

Matt. 11:29 (NASB)

U Look among the nations and watch—be *utterly* astounded! For I will work a work in your days which you would not believe, though it were told you.

Hab. 1:5

Very truly, I tell you, the one who believes in me will also do the works that I do and, in fact, will do greater works than these, because I am going to the Father.

John 14:12 (NRSV)

While the earth remains, seedtime and harvest, cold and heat, winter and summer, and day and night shall not cease.

Gen. 8:22

X Behold, My Servant shall deal prudently, He shall be *exalted* and *extolled*, and be very high.

Isa. 52:13 (KJV)

You shall call, and the Lord will answer; you shall cry, and He will say, "Here I am."

Isa. 58:9a

Z The ransomed of the Lord shall return, and come to *Zion* with singing; everlasting joy shall be upon their heads; they shall obtain joy and gladness, and sorrow and sighing shall flee away.

Isa. 35:10 (NRSV)

Redemption

All we like sheep have gone astray; we have turned, every one, to his own way; and the Lord has laid on Him the iniquity of us all.

Isa. 53:6

Being justified freely by His grace through the redemption that is in Christ Jesus.

Rom. 3:24 (KJV)

Christ has redeemed us from the curse of the law, having become a curse for us (for it is written, "Cursed is everyone who hangs on a tree").

Gal. 3:13

Do not grieve the Holy Spirit of God, by whom you were sealed for the day of redemption.

Eph. 4:30 (NASB)

Even we ourselves groan within ourselves, waiting eagerly for our adoption as sons and daughters, the redemption of our body.

Rom. 8:23b (NASB)

For this reason He is the Mediator of the new covenant, by means of death, for the redemption of the transgressions under the first covenant, that those who are called may receive the promise of the eternal inheritance.

Heb. 9:15

God forbid that I should boast except in the cross of our Lord Jesus Christ, by whom the world has been crucified to me, and I to the world.

Gal. 6:14

He was wounded for our transgressions, He was bruised for our iniquities: the chastisement of our peace was upon Him; and with His stripes we are healed.

Isa. 53:5 (KJV)

In Him we have redemption through His blood, the forgiveness of sins, in accordance with the riches of God's grace.

Eph. 1:7 (NIV)

Just as many were astonished at you, so His visage was marred more than any man, and His form more than the sons of men.

Isa. 52:14

Knowing that you were not redeemed with perishable things like silver or gold from your futile way of life inherited from your forefathers, but with precious blood, as of a lamb unblemished and spotless, the blood of Christ.

1 Peter 1:18, 19 (NASB)

Looking for that blessed hope, and the glorious appearing of the great God and our Saviour Jesus Christ; who gave Himself for us, that He might redeem us from all iniquity, and purify unto Himself a peculiar people, zealous of good works.

Titus 2:13, 14 (KJV)

My little children, I am writing these things to you so that you may not sin. And if anyone sins, we have an Advocate with the Father, Jesus Christ the righteous.

1 John 2:1 (NASB)

Not with the blood of goats or calves, but with His own blood He entered the Most Holy Place once for all, having obtained eternal redemption.

Heb. 9:12

Oh give thanks to the Lord, for He is good! For His mercy endures forever. Let the redeemed of the Lord say so, whom He has redeemed from the hand of the enemy.

Ps. 107:1, 2

P In all their distress He was distressed, and the angel of His *presence* saved them; in His love and in His mercy He redeemed them, and He lifted them and carried them all the days of old.

Isa. 63:9 (NASB)

Q The Lord your God in your midst, the Mighty One, will save; he will rejoice over you with gladness, he will *quiet* you with His love, He will rejoice over you with singing.

Zeph. 3:17

R Your Maker is your husband, the Lord of hosts is His name; and your *Redeemer* is the Holy One of Israel; He is called the God of the whole earth.

Isa. 54:5

Surely He has borne our griefs and carried our sorrows; yet we esteemed Him stricken, smitten of God, and afflicted.

Isa. 53:4

They sang a new song, saying: "Worthy are You to take the scroll and to break its seals; for You were slaughtered, and You purchased people for God with Your blood from every tribe language, and people, and nation."

Rev. 5:9 (NASB)

Upholding all things by the word of His power, when He had by Himself purged our sins, sat down on the right hand of the Majesty on high.

Heb. 1:3b (KJV)

Verily, verily, I say unto you, He that heareth my word, and believeth on Him that sent Me, hath everlasting life, and shall not come into condemnation; but is passed from death into life.

John 5:24 (KJV)

When the fullness of the time had come, God sent forth His Son, born of a woman, born under the law, to redeem those who were under the law, that we might receive the adoption as sons.

Gal. 4:4, 5

X I determined not to know anything among you *except* Jesus Christ and Him crucified.

1 Cor. 2:2

You, O Lord, are our Father; our Redeemer from of old is Your name.

Isa. 63:16b (NRSV)

Z The ransomed of the Lord shall return, and come to **Zion** with singing; everlasting joy shall be upon their heads; they shall obtain joy and gladness, and sorrow and sighing shall flee away.

Isa. 35:10 (NRSV)

Righteousness

As righteousness leads to life, so he who pursues evil pursues it to his own death.

Prov. 11:19

Blessed are those who hunger and thirst for righteousness, for they will be filled.

Matt. 5:6 (NRSV)

Christ is the end of the Law for righteousness to everyone who believes.

Rom. 10:4 (NASB)

Do not present your members as instruments of unrighteousness to sin, but present yourselves to God as being alive from the dead, and your members as instruments of righteousness to God.

Rom. 6:13

Even if you should suffer for the sake of righteousness, you are blessed. And do not fear their intimidation, and do not be in dread.

1 Peter 3:14 (NASB)

F The *fruit* of the righteous is a tree of life, and he who is wise gains souls.

Prov. 11:30 (NASB)

God be thanked that though you were slaves of sin, yet you obeyed from the heart that form of doctrine to which you were delivered. And having been set free from sin, you became slaves of righteousness.

Rom. 6:17, 18

He who follows righteousness and mercy finds life, righteousness, and honor.

Prov. 21:21

I have been young and now I am old, yet I have not seen the righteous forsaken or his descendants begging for bread.

Ps. 37:25 (NASB)

Jesus answered and said to him [John the Baptist], "Permit it to be so now, for thus it is fitting for us to fulfill all righteousness." Then He allowed Him.

Matt. 3:15

Keep justice, and do righteousness, for My salvation is about to come, and My righteousness to be revealed.

Isa. 56:1

Little children, make sure no one deceives you; the one who practices righteousness is righteous, just as He is righteous.

1 John 3:7 (NASB)

My tongue shall speak of Your word, for all Your commandments are righteousness.

Ps. 119:172

Nevertheless we, according to His promise, look for new heavens and a new earth in which righteousness dwells.

2 Pet. 3:13

Open the gates of righteousness to me; I will enter through them, I will give thanks to the Lord.

Ps. 118:19 (NASB)

Put on the whole armor of God, that you may be able to stand against the wiles of the devil…. Stand therefore, having girded your waist with truth, having put on the breastplate of righteousness.

Eph. 6:11, 14

Q The work of righteousness shall be peace; and the effect of righteousness *quietness* and assurance for ever.

Isa. 32:17 (KJV)

Rain down, you heavens, from above, and let the skies pour down righteousness; let the earth open, let them bring forth salvation, and let righteousness spring up together. I, the Lord, have created it.

Isa. 45:8

Seek first the kingdom of God and His righteousness, and all these things shall be added to you.

Matt. 6:33

Those who are wise shall shine like the brightness of the sky, and those who turn many to righteousness, like the stars forever and ever.

Dan. 12:3 (NRSV)

Upon the wicked He will rain coals; fire and brimstone and a burning wind shall be the portion of their cup. For the Lord is righteous, He loves righteousness; His countenance beholds the upright.

Ps. 11:6, 7

Verily I say unto you, that the publicans and the harlots go into the kingdom of God before you. For John came unto you in the way of righteousness, and ye believed him not: but the publicans and harlots believed him.

Matt. 21:31b, 32a (KJV)

When the righteous turn away from their righteousness and commit iniquity, they shall die for it; for the iniquity that they have committed they shall die.

Ezek. 18:26 (NRSV)

X Righteousness *exalts* a nation, but sin is a reproach to any people.

Prov. 14:34

Your righteousness is an everlasting righteousness, and Your law is truth.

Ps. 119:142

Z I bring near My righteousness, it is not far off; and My salvation will not delay. And I will grant salvation in *Zion*, and My glory for Israel.

Isa. 46:13 (NASB)

Sin

All have sinned and fall short of the glory of God.

Rom. 3:23 (NIV)

Blessed is he whose transgression is forgiven, whose sin is covered.

Ps. 32:1

Consider Him who endured such hostility by sinners against Himself, so that you will not grow weary and lose heart.

Heb. 12:3 (NASB)

Do not offer any part of yourself to sin as an instrument of wickedness, but rather offer yourselves to God as those who have been brought from death to life; and offer every part of yourself to Him as an instrument of righteousness.

Rom. 6:13 (NIV)

Everyone proud in heart is an abomination to the Lord; though they join forces, none will go unpunished.

Prov. 16:5

For as by one man's disobedience many were made sinners, so also by one Man's obedience many will be made righteous.

Rom. 5:19

God demonstrates His own love toward us, in that while we were still sinners, Christ died for us.

Rom. 5:8 (NASB)

He who sins is of the devil, for the devil has sinned from the beginning. For this purpose the Son of God was manifested, that He might destroy the works of the devil.

1 John 3:8

If we confess our sins, He is faithful and just to forgive us our sins and to cleanse us from all unrighteousness.

1 John 1:9

Just as David also speaks of the blessing of the person to whom God credits righteousness apart from works: "Blessed are those whose lawless deeds are forgiven, and whose sins are covered. Blessed is the man whose sin the Lord will not take into account."

Rom. 4:6–8 (NASB)

Knowing this, that our old self was crucified with Him, in order that our body of sin might be done away with, so that we would no longer be slaves to sin.

Rom. 6:6 (NASB)

Let him know that he who turns a sinner from the error of his way will save a soul from death and cover a multitude of sins.

James 5:20

My little children, I am writing these things to you so that you may not sin. And if anyone sins, we have an Advocate with the Father, Jesus Christ the righteous.

1 John 2:1 (NASB)

No more shall every man teach his neighbor, and every man his brother, saying, "Know the Lord," for they shall all know me, from the least of them to the greatest of them, says the Lord. For I will forgive their iniquity, and their sin I will remember no more."

Jer. 31:34

Our wrongful acts have multiplied before You, and our sins have testified against us; for our wrongful acts are with us, and we know our wrongdoings.

Isa. 59:12 (NASB)

Pride goes before destruction, and a haughty spirit before a fall.

Prov. 16:18 (NRSV)

Q They shall go out and look at the dead bodies of the people who have rebelled against Me; for their worm shall not die, their fire shall not be *quenched*, and they shall be an abhorrence to all flesh.

Isa. 66:24 (NRSV)

Reckon yourselves to be dead indeed to sin, but alive to God in Christ Jesus our Lord.

Rom. 6:11b

Sin shall not have dominion over you, for you are not under law but under grace.

Rom. 6:14

To him who knows to do good and does not do it, to him it is sin.

James 4:17

Until the law sin was in the world: but sin is not imputed when there is no law.

Rom. 5:13 (KJV)

V Why do You show me iniquity, and cause me to see trouble? For plundering and *violence* are before me; there is strife, and contention arises.

Hab. 1:3

Whoever abides in Him does not sin. Whoever sins has neither seen Him nor known Him.

1 John 3:6

X He is the one whom God *exalted* to His right hand as a Prince and a Savior, to grant repentance to Israel, and forgiveness of sins.

Acts 5:31 (NASB)

You know that He appeared in order to take away sins; and in Him there is no sin.

1 John 3:5 (NASB)

Zacchaeus stood up and said to the Lord, "Look, Lord! Here and now I give half of my possessions to the poor, and if I have cheated anybody out of anything, I will pay back four times the amount."

Luke 19:8 (NIV)

The Christian Life

As you therefore have received Christ Jesus the Lord, so walk in Him.

Col. 2:6

Be kindly affectioned one to another with brotherly love; in honour preferring one another.

Rom. 12:10 (KJV)

Continue earnestly in prayer, being vigilant in it with thanksgiving.

Col. 4:2

Do all things without complaining and disputing, that you may become blameless and harmless, children of God without fault in the midst of a crooked and perverse generation, among whom you shine as lights in the world.

Phil. 2:14, 15

Enter into His gates with thanksgiving, and into His courts with praise: be thankful unto Him, and bless His name

Ps. 100:4 (KJV)

Fight the good fight of the faith; take hold of the eternal life, to which you were called and for which you made the good confession in the presence of many witnesses.

1 Tim. 6:12 (NRSV)

Grow in grace, and in the knowledge of our Lord and Saviour Jesus Christ. To Him be glory both now and for ever. Amen.

2 Pet. 3:18 (KJV)

Honour all men. Love the brotherhood. Fear God. Honour the king.

1 Peter 2:17 (KJV)

If it is possible, as much as depends on you, live peaceably with all men.

Rom. 12:18

Judge not, that you be not judged.

Matt. 7:1

Keep your tongue from evil, and your lips from speaking deceit.

Ps. 34:13

Let us not grow weary while doing good, for in due season we shall reap if we do not lose heart.

Gal. 6:9

Moreover it is required in stewards that one be found faithful.

1 Cor. 4:2

Now you also, rid yourselves of all of them: anger, wrath, malice, slander, and obscene speech from your mouth.

Col. 3:8 (NASB)

Only, live your life in a manner worthy of the gospel of Christ, so that, whether I come and see you or am absent and hear about you, I will know that you are standing firm in one spirit, striving side by side with one mind for the faith of the gospel.

Phil. 1:27 (NRSV)

Put on the whole armor of God, so that you may be able to stand against the wiles of the devil.

Eph. 6:11 (NRSV)

Quench not the Spirit.

1 Thess. 5:19 (KJV)

Rejoice with those who rejoice, and weep with those who weep.

Rom. 12:15

Set your mind on things above, not on things on the earth.

Col. 3:2

Test all things; hold fast what is good.

1 Thess. 5:21

U Endeavoring to keep the *unity* of the Spirit in the bond of peace.

Eph. 4:3

V Abide in Me as I abide in you. Just as the branch cannot bear fruit by itself unless it abides in the *vine*, neither can you unless you abide in Me.

John 15:4 (NRSV)

Whatever you do in word or deed, do everything in the name of the Lord Jesus, giving thanks through Him to God the Father.

Col. 3:17 (NASB)

X *Exhort* one another every day, as long as it is called "today," so that none of you may be hardened by the deceitfulness of sin.

Heb. 3:13 (NRSV)

You, O man of God, flee these things and pursue righteousness, godliness, faith, love, patience, gentleness.

1 Tim. 6:11

Z Even so you, since you are *zealous* for spiritual gifts, let it be for the edification of the church that you seek to excel.

1 Cor. 14:12

The Shepherd and His Sheep

As the Father knows Me, even so I know the Father; and I lay down My life for the sheep.

John 10:15

Behold, I send you out as sheep in the midst of wolves. Therefore be wise as serpents and harmless as doves.

Matt. 10:16

Christ also suffered for sins once for all time, the just for the unjust, so that He might bring us to God, having been put to death in the flesh, but made alive in the Spirit.

1 Peter 3:18 (NASB)

Do not be afraid, little flock, for it is your Father's good pleasure to give you the kingdom.

Luke 12:32 (NRSV)

Even so, it is not the will of your Father in heaven that one of these little ones should perish.

Matt. 18:14

For the Lamb who is in the midst of the throne will shepherd them and lead them to living fountains of waters. And God will wipe away every tear from their eyes.

Rev. 7:17

Give ear, O Shepherd of Israel, You who lead Joseph like a flock! You who are enthroned upon the cherubim, shine forth.

Ps. 80:1 (NRSV)

He makes me lie down in green pastures; He leads me beside still waters.

Ps. 23:2 (NRSV)

I am the good Shepherd; and I know My sheep, and am known by My own.

John 10:14

Jesus said to them, "You will all fall away because of Me this night, for it is written: 'I will strike the Shepherd, and the sheep of the flock will be scattered.'"

Matt. 26:31 (NASB)

Know that the Lord, He is God; it is He who has made us, and not we ourselves; we are His people and the sheep of His pasture.

Ps. 100:3

L The *Lord* is my shepherd, I shall not want.

Ps. 23:1

My sheep hear my voice. I know them, and they follow Me.

John 10:27 (NRSV)

Now may the God of peace, who brought back from the dead our Lord Jesus, the great Shepherd of the sheep, by the blood of the eternal covenant, make you complete in everything good so that you may do His will.

Heb. 13:20, 21a (NRSV)

Other sheep I have, which are not of this fold: them also I must bring, and they shall hear My voice; and there will be one fold, and one Shepherd.

John 10:16 (KJV)

Prophesy against the shepherds of Israel, prophesy and say to them, "Thus says the Lord God to the shepherds: 'Woe to the shepherds of Israel who feed themselves! Should not the shepherds feed the flocks?'"

Ezek. 34:2b

Q He will not *quarrel*, nor cry out; nor will anyone hear His voice in the streets.

Matt. 12:19 (NASB)

R He *restores* my soul; He leads me in the paths of righteousness for His name's sake.

Ps. 23:3

Shepherd the flock of God which is among you, serving as overseers, not by compulsion but willingly, not for dishonest gain but eagerly.

1 Peter 5:2

The Lord God says this: "Behold, I Myself will search for My sheep and look after them."

Ezek. 34:11 (NASB)

U My soul follows close behind You; Your right hand *upholds* me.

Ps. 63:8

Verily, verily, I say unto you, I am the door of the sheep.

John 10:7 (KJV)

What do you think? If a shepherd has a hundred sheep, and one of them has gone astray, does he not leave the ninety-nine on the mountains and go in search of the one that went astray?

Matt. 18:12 (NRSV)

X Not lording it over those entrusted to you, but being *examples* to the flock. And when the Chief Shepherd appears, you will receive the crown of glory that will never fade away.

1 Peter 5:3, 4 (NIV)

Yea, though I walk through the valley of the shadow of death, I will fear no evil; for You are with me; Your rod and Your staff, they comfort me.

Ps. 23:4

Z O my people, who live in *Zion*, do not be afraid of the Assyrians when they beat you with a rod and lift up their staff against you as the Egyptians did.... The Lord of hosts will wield a whip against them, as when he struck Midian at the rock of Oreb; his staff will be over the sea, and He will lift it as He did in Egypt.

Isa. 10:24, 26 (NRSV)

Trust

As for me, I trust in You, Lord, I say, "You are my God."

Ps. 31:14 (NASB)

Blessed is that man who makes the Lord his trust, and does not respect the proud, nor such as turn aside to lies.

Ps. 40:4

Commit your way to the Lord, trust also in Him, and He shall bring it to pass.

Ps. 37:5

Delight yourself in the Lord; and He will give you the desires of your heart.

Ps. 37:4 (NASB)

Evildoers shall be cut off: but those that wait upon the Lord, they shall inherit the earth.

Ps. 37:9 (KJV)

Fear not, for I am with you; be not dismayed, for I am your God. I will strengthen you, yes, I will help you, I will uphold you with My righteous right hand.

Isa. 41:10

God is our refuge and strength, a very present help in trouble.

Ps. 46:1 (KJV)

How precious is Your loving kindness, O God! Therefore the children of men put their trust under the shadow of Your wings.

Ps. 36:7

It is better to trust in the Lord than to put confidence in man.

Ps. 118:8 (KJV)

Jesus answered again and said to them, "Children, how hard it is for those who trust in riches to enter the kingdom of God!"

Mark 10:24b

Keep my soul, and deliver me; let me not be ashamed, for I put my trust in You.

Ps. 25:20

L The *Lord* is my strength and my shield; my heart trusts in Him, and I am helped.

Ps. 28:7a (NASB)

Many sorrows shall be to the wicked; but he who trusts in the Lord, mercy shall surround him.

Ps. 32:10

None of them who trust in Him shall be desolate.

Ps. 34:22b (KJV)

Oh, taste and see that the Lord is good; blessed is the man who trusts in Him!

Ps. 34:8

Preserve me, O God, for in You I put my trust.

Ps. 16:1

Q No one calls for justice, nor does any plead for truth. They trust in empty words and speak lies; they conceive evil and bring forth *iniquity.*

Isa. 59:4

Rest in the Lord and wait patiently for Him; do not get upset because of one who is successful in his way, because of the person who carries out wicked schemes.

Ps. 37:7 (NASB)

So are the paths of all who forget God; and the hope of the godless will perish, his confidence is fragile, and his trust is a spider's web.

Job 8:13, 14 (NASB)

Trust in the Lord with all your heart, and lean not on your own understanding.

Prov. 3:5

U The righteous shall be glad in the Lord, and shall trust in him; and all the *upright* in heart shall glory.

Ps. 64:10 (KJV)

Vindicate me, O Lord, for I have walked in my integrity, and I have trusted in the Lord without wavering.

Ps. 26:1 (NRSV)

Whenever I am afraid, I will trust in You.

Ps. 56:3

X You are my God, and I will praise You; You are my God, and I will *exalt* You.

Ps. 118:28 (NIV)

You are He who brought me forth from the womb; You made me trust when upon my mother's breasts.

Ps. 22:9 (NASB)

Z Those who trust in the Lord are like Mount *Zion,* which cannot be moved, but abides forever.

Ps. 125:1

Wisdom

A wise man will hear and increase learning, and a man of understanding will attain wise counsel.

Prov. 1:5

By pride comes nothing but strife, but with the well-advised is wisdom.

Prov. 13:10

Counsel is mine, and sound wisdom: I am understanding; I have strength.

Prov. 8:14 (KJV)

Do not be wise in your own eyes; fear the Lord and shun evil.

Prov. 3:7 (NIV)

Even fools are thought wise if they keep silent, and discerning if they hold their tongues.

Prov. 17:28 (NIV)

For the Lord gives wisdom; from His mouth come knowledge and understanding. He holds success in store for the upright; He is a shield to those whose walk is blameless.

Prov. 2:6 ,7 (NIV)

Give instruction to a wise man, and he will be yet wiser: teach a just man, and he will increase in learning.

Prov. 9:9 (KJV)

He who gets wisdom loves his own soul; he who keeps understanding will find good.

Prov. 19:8

J It is a *joy* for the *just* to do *justice*, but destruction will come to the workers of iniquity.

Prov. 21:15

Keep your heart with all vigilance, for from it flow the springs of life.

Prov. 4:23 (NRSV)

Long life is in her right hand; in her left hand are riches and honor.

Prov. 3:16 (NRSV)

My fruit is better than gold, yes, than fine gold, and my revenue than choice silver.

Prov. 8:19

Now therefore, listen to me, my children, for blessed are those who keep my ways.

Prov. 8:32

Open rebuke is better than secret love.

Prov. 27:5 (KJV)

Pride goes before destruction, a haughty spirit before a fall.

Prov. 16:18 (NIV)

Q He who passes by and meddles in a *quarrel* not his own is like one who takes a dog by the ears.

Prov. 26:17

Receive my instruction, and not silver; and knowledge rather than choice gold. For wisdom is better than rubies; and all the things that may be desired are not to be compared to it.

Prov. 8:10, 11 (KJV)

Say to wisdom, "You are my sister," and call understanding your nearest kin.

Prov. 7:4

The fear of the Lord is the beginning of wisdom: and the knowledge of the Holy is understanding.

Prov. 9:10 (KJV)

Understanding is a fountain of life to those who have it, but the discipline of fools is foolishness.

Prov. 16:22 (NASB)

V When you make a *vow* to God, do not delay to pay it; for He has no pleasure in fools. Pay what you have *vowed*—Better not to *vow* than to *vow* and not pay.

Eccles. 5:4, 5

Wisdom is the principal thing; therefore get wisdom. And in all your getting, get understanding.

Prov. 4:7

X Exalt her, and she will promote you; she will bring you honor, when you embrace her.

Prov. 4:8

Y Rejoice, *young* man, while you are *young*, and let your heart cheer you in the days of your *youth*. Follow the inclination of your heart and in the desire of your eyes, but know that for all these things God will bring you into judgment.

Eccles. 11:9 (NRSV)

Z Do not let your heart envy sinners, but always be *zealous* for the fear of the Lord. There is surely a future hope for you, and your hope will not be cut off.

Prov. 23:17, 18 (NIV)

Old Testament Books

Isaiah

All we like sheep have gone astray; we have turned, every one, to his own way; and the Lord has laid on Him the iniquity of us all.

Isa. 53:6

Behold, God is my salvation, I will trust and not be afraid; for the Lord God is my strength and song, and He has become my salvation.

Isa. 12:2 (NASB)

Come now, and let us debate your case", says the Lord, "Though your sins are as scarlet, they will be as white as snow; though they are red like crimson, they shall be like wool."

Isa. 1:18 (NASB)

Doubtless You are our Father.... You, O Lord, are our Father; our Redeemer from Everlasting is Your name.

Isa. 63:16

Even to your old age, I am He, and even to gray hairs I will carry you! I have made, and I will bear; even I will carry, and I will deliver you.

Isa. 46:4

Fear not, for I am with you; be not dismayed, for I am your God. I will strengthen you, yes, I will help you, I will uphold you with My righteous right hand.

Isa. 41:10

Grass withers, the flower fades, but the word of our God stands forever.

Isa. 40:8 (NASB)

He will swallow up death forever, and the Lord God will wipe away tears from all faces; the rebuke of His people He will take away from all the earth; for the Lord has spoken.

Isa. 25:8

I, only I, am the Lord, and there is no Savior besides Me.

Isa. 43:11 (NASB)

Justice will dwell in the wilderness, and righteousness abide in the fruitful field.

Isa. 32:16 (NRSV)

Keep justice, and do righteousness, for My salvation is about to come, and My righteousness to be revealed.

Isa. 56:1

Learn to do good; seek justice, rebuke the oppressor; defend the fatherless, plead for the widow.

Isa. 1:17

My thoughts are not your thoughts, nor are your ways My ways," declares the Lord.

Isa. 55:8 (NASB)

No weapon formed against you shall prosper, and every tongue which rises against you in judgment you shall condemn. This is the heritage of the servants of the Lord, and their righteousness is from me," says the Lord.

Isa. 54:17

O Lord, you are my God; I will exalt you, I will praise your name; for you have done wonderful things, plans formed of old, faithful and sure.

Isa. 25:1 (NRSV)

Precept must be upon precept, precept upon precept, line upon line, line upon line, here a little, there a little.

Isa. 28:10

Q Thus said the Lord God, the Holy One of Israel: In returning and rest you shall be saved; in *quietness* and in trust shall be your strength. But you refused.

Isa. 30:15 (NRSV)

Remember the former things of old, for I am God, and there is no other; I am God, and there is none like Me.

Isa. 46:9

Say to the righteous that it will go well with them, for they will eat the fruit of their actions.

Isa. 3:10 (NASB)

Those who wait on the Lord shall renew their strength; they shall mount up with wings like eagles, they shall run and not be weary, they shall walk and not faint.

Isa. 40:31

Unto us a Child is born, unto us a Son is given; and the government will be upon His shoulder. And His name shall be called Wonderful, Counselor, Mighty God, Everlasting Father, Prince of Peace.

Isa. 9:6

Violence will not be heard again in your land, nor devastation or destruction within your borders; but you will call your walls salvation, and your gates praise.

Isa. 60:18 (NASB)

When you pass through the waters, I will be with you; and through the rivers, they will not overthrow you. When you walk through the fire, you will not be scorched, nor will the flame burn you.

Isa. 43:2 (NASB)

X The Lord is *exalted*, for He dwells on high; he has filled Zion with justice and righteousness.

Isa. 33:5

You will keep him in perfect peace, whose mind is stayed on You, because he trusts in You.

Isa. 26:3

Zion shall be redeemed by justice, and those in her who repent, by righteousness.

Isa. 1:27 (NRSV)

Jeremiah and Lamentations

Am I a God who is near," declares the Lord, "and not a God far off?"

Jer. 23:23 (NASB)

Behold, I am the Lord, the God of all flesh; is anything too difficult for Me?

Jer. 32:27 (NASB)

Call to Me, and I will answer you, and show you great and mighty things, which you do not know.

Jer. 33:3

Do not be afraid of them, for I am with you to save you," declares the Lord.

Jer. 1:8 (NASB)

Even the stork in the sky knows her seasons; and the turtledove, the swallow, and the crane keep to the time of their migration, but My people do not know the judgment of the Lord.

Jer. 8:7 (NASB)

For I know the thoughts that I think toward you, says the Lord, thoughts of peace and not evil, to give you a future and a hope.

Jer. 29:11

Give heed to me, O Lord, and listen to what my adversaries say!

Jer. 18:19 (NRSV)

Heal me, O Lord, and I shall be healed; save me, and I shall be saved, for You are my praise.

Jer. 17:14

I, the Lord, search the heart, I test the mind, to give each person according to his ways, according to the results of his deeds.

Jer. 17:10 (NASB)

Just as I have brought all this great calamity on this people, so I will bring on them all the good that I have promised them.

Jer. 32:42b

Know therefore and see that it is evil and bitter for you to abandon the Lord your God, and the fear of Me is not in you," declares the Lord God of armies.

Jer. 2:19b (NASB)

Let not the wise man glory in his wisdom, let not the mighty man glory in his might, nor the rich man glory in his riches; but let him that glories glory in this, that he understands and knows Me, that I am the Lord, exercising lovingkindness, judgment, and righteousness in the earth. For in these I delight," says the Lord.

Jer. 9:23, 24

My eyes flow unceasingly, without stopping, until the Lord looks down and sees from heaven.

Lam. 3:49, 50 (NASB)

No longer will they teach their neighbor, or say to one another, 'Know the Lord,' because they will all know Me, from the least of them to the greatest," declares the Lord. "For I will forgive their wickedness and will remember their sins no more."

Jer. 31:34 (NIV)

Obey My voice, and I will be your God, and you shall be My people. And walk in all the ways that I have commanded you, that it may be well with you.

Jer. 7:23b

P The *Portion* of Jacob is not like them, for He is the Maker of all things, and Israel is the tribe of His inheritance; the Lord of hosts is His name.

Jer. 10:16

Q It is good that one should hope and wait *quietly* for the salvation of the Lord.

Lam. 3:26

Return, you backsliding children, and I will heal your backslidings.

Jer. 3:22a

Stand in the gate of the Lord's house and proclaim there this word, and say, 'Hear the word of the Lord, all you of Judah, who enter by these gates to worship the Lord!'

Jer. 7:2 (NASB)

Through the Lord's mercies we are not consumed, because His compassions fail not. They are new every morning; Great is Your faithfulness.

Lam. 3:22, 23

U When He *utters* His voice there is a tumult of waters in the heavens, and He makes the mist rise from the ends of the earth. He makes lightnings for the rain, and He brings the wind from His storehouses.

Jer. 51:16 (NRSV)

V Thus says the Lord: 'Again there shall be heard in this place...the *voice* of joy and the *voice* of gladness, the *voice* of the bridegroom and the *voice* of the bride, the *voice* of those who will say: "Praise the Lord of hosts, for the Lord is good, for His mercy endures forever."

Jer. 33:10a, 11

Who would not fear You, O King of the nations? For this is Your rightful due. For among all the wise men of the nations, and in all their kingdoms, there is none like You.

Jer. 10:7

X In those days and at that time I will make a righteous Branch of David sprout; and He shall *execute* justice and righteousness on the earth.

Jer. 33:15 (NASB)

You will seek Me and find Me when you search for Me with all your heart.

Jer. 29:13 (NASB)

Z I have likened the daughter of *Zion* to a lovely and delicate woman.

Jer. 6:2

Job

As for me, I would seek God, and to God I would commit my cause.

Job 5:8

Behold, happy is the man whom God disciplines, so do not reject the discipline of the Almighty.

Job 5:17 (NASB)

Can you search out the deep things of God? Can you find out the limits of the Almighty?

Job 11:7

Does God pervert justice? Does the Almighty pervert what is right?

Job 8:3 (NIV)

E The *ear* tests words as the tongue tastes food.

Job 34:3 (NIV)

For His eyes are on the ways of man, and He sees all his steps.

Job 34:21

God is wise in heart and mighty in strength. Who has hardened himself against Him and prospered?

Job 9:4

He knows the way I take; when He has put me to the test, I will come out as gold.

Job 23:10 (NASB)

I know that my Redeemer lives, and that at the last He will stand upon the earth.

Job 19:25 (NRSV)

Job answered the Lord and said, "I know that You can do all things, and that no plan is impossible for you.

Job 42:1, 2 (NASB)

K After my skin is destroyed, this I *know,* that in my flesh I shall see God.

Job 19:26

Let us choose for ourselves what is right; let us understand among ourselves what is good.

Job 34:4 (NASB)

My lips will not speak falsehood, and my tongue will not utter deceit.

Job 27:4 (NRSV)

Naked I came from my mother's womb, and naked I shall return there. The Lord gave and the Lord has taken away. Blessed be the name of the Lord.

Job 1:21 (NASB)

Oh, that one might plead for a man with God, as a man pleads for his neighbor!

Job 16:21

P My hands have been free from violence and my *prayer* is pure.

Job 16:17 (NIV)

Q When He gives *quietness,* who then can make trouble? And when He hides His face, who then can see Him?

Job 34:29a

Receive instruction from His mouth, and lay up His words in your heart.

Job 22:22 (NRSV)

Surely even now my witness is in heaven, and my evidence is on high.

Job 16:19

Though He slay me, yet will I trust Him. Even so, I will defend my own ways before Him.

Job 13:15

Upon whom does His light not rise?

Job 25:3b

V God thunders wondrously with His *voice*, doing great things which we do not comprehend.

Job 37:5 (NASB)

Wisdom is with the aged, and with long life comes understanding.

Job 12:12 (NASB)

X Behold, God is *exalted* by His power; who teaches like Him?

Job 36:22

You have granted me life and goodness; and Your care has guarded my spirit.

Job 10:12 (NASB)

Zophar the Naamathite replied… "Surely you know how it has been from of old, ever since mankind was placed on the earth … that the mirth of the wicked is brief, the joy of the godless lasts but a moment."

Job 20:1, 4, 5 (NIV)

Minor Prophets

All the nations may walk in the name of their gods, but we will walk in the name of the Lord our God for ever and ever.

Mic. 4:5 (NIV)

Behold, I will save My people from the land of the east and from the land of the west.

Zech. 8:7b

Can two walk together, unless they are agreed?

Amos 3:3

Do not oppress the widow or the orphan, the stranger or the poor; and do not devise evil in your hearts against one another.

Zech. 7:10 (NASB)

Every morning He brings His justice to light; He does not fail. But the criminal knows no shame.

Zeph. 3:5b (NASB)

From the rising of the sun even to its setting, My name shall be great among the nations.

Mal. 1:11a (NASB)

God saw their works, that they turned from their evil way; and God relented from the disaster that He had said he would bring upon them, and He did not do it.

Jonah 3:10

He has shown you, O mortal, what is good. And what does the Lord require of you? To act justly and to love mercy and to walk humbly with your God.

Mic. 6:8 (NIV)

I will betroth you to Me forever; yes, I will betroth you to Me in righteousness and in justice, in favor and in compassion, and I will betroth you to Me in faithfulness, then you will know the Lord.

Hosea 2:19, 20 (NASB)

Jerusalem shall be called the City of Truth, the Mountain of the Lord of hosts, the Holy Mountain.

Zech. 8:3b

K My people are destroyed for lack of *knowledge*; because you have rejected *knowledge*, I reject you from being a priest to Me. And since you have forgotten the law of your God, I will also forget your children.

Hosea 4:6 (NRSV)

Let none of you devise evil in your heart against another, and do not love perjury; for all these things are what I hate,' declares the Lord.

Zech. 8:17 (NASB)

Many nations will join themselves to the Lord on that day and will become My people. Then I will dwell in your midst, and you will know that the Lord of armies has sent Me to you.

Zech. 2:11 (NASB)

Not by might nor by power, but by My Spirit, says the Lord of hosts.

Zech. 4:6b

Observe mercy and justice, and wait on your God continually.

Hosea 12:6b

Proclaim, saying, 'This is what the Lord or armies says: "I am exceedingly jealous for Jerusalem and Zion."

Zech. 1:14b (NASB)

Q The mountains *quake* before Him, and the hills melt; the earth heaves before Him, and the world and all who live in it.

Nah.1:5 (NRSV)

Rend your heart and not your garments. Return to the Lord your God, for He is gracious and compassionate, slow to anger and abounding in love, and He relents from sending calamity.

Joel 2:13 (NIV)

Sow for yourselves righteousness; reap in mercy, break up the fallow ground, for it is time to seek the Lord, till He comes and rains righteousness on you.

Hosea 10:12

They shall be mine," says the Lord of hosts, "On the day that I make them My jewels. And I will spare them as a man spares his own son who serves him."

Mal. 3:17

Until He pleads my case and executes justice for me. He will bring me forth to the light; I will see His righteousness.

Mic. 7:9b

V They shall all sit under their own *vines* and under their own fig trees, and no one shall make them afraid; for the mouth of the Lord of hosts has spoken.

Mic. 4:4 (NRSV)

When my soul fainted within me, I remembered the Lord; and my prayer went up to You, into Your holy temple.

Jonah 2:7

X *Execute* true justice, show mercy and compassion everyone to his brother.

Zech. 7:9b

You, Bethlehem Ephrathah, though you are small among the clans of Judah, out of you will come for Me One who will be ruler over Israel, whose origins are from of old, from ancient times.

Mic. 5:2 (NIV)

Z 'I am *zealous* for *Zion* with great *zeal*; with great fervor I am *zealous* for her.'

Zech. 8:2

Proverbs and Ecclesiastes

A soft answer turns away wrath, but a harsh word stirs up anger.

Prov. 15:1

Better is a little with the fear of the Lord than great treasure and trouble with it.

Prov. 15:16 (NRSV)

Commit your works to the Lord, and your plans will be established.

Prov. 16:3 (NASB)

Do not be wise in your own eyes; fear the Lord and depart from evil.

Prov. 3:7

Every word of God is pure; He is a shield to those who put their trust in Him.

Prov. 30:5

Foolishness is joy to one who lacks sense, but a person of understanding walks straight.

Prov. 15:21 (NASB)

Go to the ant, you sluggard; consider its ways and be wise!

Prov. 6:6 (NIV)

He who is slow to anger is better than the mighty, and he who rules his spirit than he who takes a city.

Prov.16:32

In all your ways acknowledge Him, and He shall direct your paths.

Prov. 3:6

J It is a *joy* for the *just* to do *justice*, but destruction will come to the workers of iniquity.

Prov. 21:15

Keep your heart with all vigilance, for from it flow the springs of life.

Prov. 4:23 (NRSV)

Let not mercy and truth forsake you; bind them around your neck, write them on the tablet of your heart.

Prov. 3:3

My son, hear the instruction of your father, and do not forsake the law of your mother.

Prov. 1:8

No harm overtakes the righteous, but the wicked have their fill of trouble.

Prov. 12:21 (NIV)

One who turns away his ear from hearing the law, even his prayer is an abomination.

Prov. 28:9

Ponder the path of your feet, and let all your ways be established.

Prov. 4:26

Q A *quick-tempered* person does foolish things, and the one who devises evil schemes is hated.

Prov. 14:17 (NIV)

Remember also your Creator in the days of your youth, before the evil days come and the years approach when you will say, "I have no pleasure in them."

Eccles. 12:1 (NASB)

So I saw that there is nothing better for a person than to enjoy their work, because that is their lot. For who can bring them to see what will happen after them?

Eccles. 3:22 (NIV)

To everything there is a season, a time for every purpose under heaven.

Eccles. 3:1

Understanding is a fountain of life to those who have it, but the discipline of fools is foolishness.

Prov. 16:22 (NASB)

Vanity of vanities," says the Preacher, "all is vanity."

Eccles. 12:8

Wisdom is the principal thing; therefore get wisdom. And in all your getting, get understanding.

Prov. 4:7

X *Exalt* her [wisdom], and she will promote you; she will bring you honor, when you embrace her.

Prov. 4:8

Y Rejoice, *young* man, during your childhood, and let your heart be pleasant during the days of young manhood. And follow the impulses of your heart and the desires of your eyes. Yet know that God will bring you to judgment for all these things.

Eccles. 11:9 (NASB)

Z The soul of a *lazy* one craves and gets nothing, but the soul of the diligent is made prosperous.

Prov. 13:4 (NASB)

Psalms

As a father has compassion on his children, so the Lord has compassion on those who fear Him; for He knows how we are formed, He remembers that we are dust.

Ps. 103:13, 14 (NIV)

Behold, the eye of the Lord is on those who fear Him, on those who hope in His mercy.

Ps. 33:18

Commit your way to the Lord, trust also in Him, and He shall bring it to pass.

Ps. 37:5

Delight yourself in the Lord; and He will give you the desires of your heart.

Ps. 37:4 (NASB)

Evening, and morning, and at noon, will I pray, and cry aloud: and He shall hear my voice.

Ps. 55:17 (KJV)

Fools say in their hearts, "There is no God." They are corrupt, they do abominable deeds; there is no one who does good.

Ps. 14:1 (NRSV)

Great peace have those who love Your law, and nothing causes them to stumble.

Ps. 119:165

He shall cover you with His feathers, and under His wings you shall take refuge; His truth shall be your shield and buckler.

Ps. 91:4

I keep the Lord always before me; because He is at my right hand, I shall not be moved.

Ps. 16:8 (NRSV)

Judgments of the Lord are true and righteous altogether.

Ps. 19:9b

Keep me as the apple of Your eye; hide me under the shadow of Your wings.

Ps. 17:8

Let the words of my mouth and the meditation of my heart be acceptable in Your sight, O Lord, my strength and my Redeemer.

Ps. 19:14

Mark the blameless man, and observe the upright; for the future of that man is peace.

Ps. 37:37

Not unto us, O Lord, not unto us, but to Your name give glory, because of Your mercy, because of Your truth.

Ps. 115:1

Oh taste and see that the Lord is good; blessed is the man who trusts in Him!

Ps. 34:8

Purge me with hyssop, and I shall be clean: wash me, and I shall be whiter than snow.

Ps. 51:7 (KJV)

Q They compassed me about like bees: they are *quenched* as the fire of thorns: for in the name of the Lord I will destroy them.

Ps. 118:12 (KJV)

Rest in the Lord and wait patiently for Him; do not get upset because of one who is successful in his way, because of the person who carries out wicked schemes.

Ps. 37:7 (NASB)

Surely goodness and mercy shall follow me all the days of my life: and I will dwell in the house of the Lord for ever.

Ps. 23:6 (KJV)

The Lord is my strength and song, and He has become my salvation.

Ps. 118:14 (NASB)

Unto the upright there arises light in the darkness; He is gracious, and full of compassion, and righteous.

Ps. 112:4

Vows made to You are binding upon me, O God; I will render praises to You.

Ps. 56:12

Whenever I am afraid, I will trust in You.

Ps. 56:3

X *Examine* me, Lord, and put me to the test; refine my mind and my heart.

Ps. 26:2 (NASB)

You will make known to me the way of life; in Your presence is fullness of joy; in Your right hand there are pleasures forever.

Ps. 16:11 (NASB)

Zion hears and rejoices, and the villages of Judah are glad because of Your judgments, Lord.

Ps. 97:8 (NIV)

New Testament Books

1ˢᵗ and 2ⁿᵈ Corinthians

As in Adam all die, so in Christ all will be made alive.

1 Cor. 15:22 (NIV)

Blessed be God, even the Father of our Lord Jesus Christ, the Father of mercies, and the God of all comfort.

2 Cor. 1:3 (KJV)

Clearly, you are an epistle of Christ, ministered by us, written not with ink but by the Spirit of the living God, not on tablets of stone but on tablets of flesh, that is, of the heart.

2 Cor. 3:3

Do you not know that your body is the temple of the Holy Spirit who is in you, whom you have from God, and you are not your own?

1 Cor. 6:19

Everyone who competes in the games goes into strict training. They do it to get a crown that will not last, but we do it to get a crown that will last forever.

1 Cor. 9:25 (NIV)

For the weapons of our warfare are not carnal, but mighty through God to the pulling down of strong holds.

2 Cor. 10:4 (KJV)

God hath chosen the foolish things of the world to confound the wise; and God hath chosen the weak things of the world to confound the things which are mighty.

1 Cor. 1:27 (KJV)

He died for all, that those who live should live no longer for themselves, but for Him who died for them and rose again.

2 Cor. 5:15

If any man be in Christ, he is a new creature: old things are passed away; behold, all things are become new.

2 Cor. 5:17 (KJV)

Judge nothing before the time, until the Lord comes, who will both bring to light the hidden things of darkness and reveal the counsels of the hearts. Then each one's praise will come from God.

1 Cor. 4:5

Knowing that He who raised up the Lord Jesus will also raise us up with Jesus, and will present us with you.

2 Cor. 4:14

Let all things be done decently and in order.

1 Cor. 14:40

My dear brothers and sisters, stand firm. Let nothing move you. Always give yourselves fully to the work of the Lord, because you know that your labor in the Lord is not in vain.

1 Cor. 15:58 (NIV)

Now abide faith, hope, love, these three; but the greatest of these is love.

1 Cor. 13:13

Our light and momentary troubles are achieving for us an eternal glory that far outweighs them all. So we fix our eyes not on what is seen, but on what is unseen, since what is seen is temporary, but what is unseen is eternal.

2 Cor. 4:17 (NIV)

Purge out the old leaven, that you may be a new lump, since you truly are unleavened. For indeed Christ, our Passover, was sacrificed for us.

1 Cor. 5:7

Q The Jews *require* a sign, and Greeks seek after wisdom: but we preach Christ crucified, unto the Jews a stumblingblock, and unto the Greeks foolishness.

1 Cor. 1:22, 23 (KJV)

Remember this: Whoever sows sparingly will also reap sparingly, and whoever sows generously will also reap generously.

2 Cor. 9:6 (NIV)

Since by man came death, by Man also came the resurrection of the dead.

1 Cor. 15:21

Though I speak with the tongues of men and of angels, but have not love, I have become sounding brass or a clanging cymbal.

1 Cor. 13:1

Unless you speak intelligible words with your tongue, how will anyone know what you are saying? You will just be speaking into the air.

1 Cor. 14:9b (NIV)

V Thanks be to God, who gives us the *victory* through our Lord Jesus Christ.

1 Cor. 15:57 (NRSV)

We are to God the aroma of Christ among those who are being saved and those who are perishing.

2 Cor. 2:15 (NIV)

X *Examine* yourselves to see whether you are in the faith; test yourselves. Do you not realize that Jesus Christ is in you?—unless, of course, you fail the test?

2 Cor. 13:5 (NIV)

You were bought at a price; therefore glorify God in your body and in your spirit, which are God's.

1 Cor. 6:20

Z Even so you, since you are *zealous* for spiritual gifts, let it be for the edification of the church that you seek to excel.

1 Cor. 14:12

Romans

As by one man's disobedience many were made sinners, so also by one Man's obedience many will be made righteous.

Rom. 5:19

Be kindly affectionate to one another with brotherly love, in honor giving preference to one another.

Rom. 12:10

Consider the goodness and severity of God: on those who fell, severity; but toward you, goodness, if you continue in His goodness. Otherwise you also will be cut off.

Rom. 11:22

Do not be conformed to this world, but be transformed by the renewing of your mind, so that you may prove what the will of God is, that which is good and acceptable and perfect.

Rom. 12:2 (NASB)

Each one of us will give an account of himself to God.

Rom. 14:12 (NASB)

For the wages of sin is death; but the gift of God is eternal life through Jesus Christ our Lord.

Rom. 6:23 (KJV)

God demonstrates His love toward us, in that while we were still sinners, Christ died for us.

Rom. 5:8

He who did not spare His own Son, but delivered Him over for us all, how will He not also with Him freely give us all things?

Rom. 8:32 (NASB)

I am not ashamed of the gospel of Christ, for it is the power of God to salvation for everyone who believes, for the Jew first and also for the Greek.

Rom. 1:16

J Therefore being *justified* by faith, we have peace with God through our Lord Jesus Christ.

Rom. 5:1 (KJV)

Knowing this, that our old self was crucified with Him, in order that our body of sin might be done away with, so that we would no longer be slaves to sin.

Rom. 6:6 (NASB)

Love does no harm to a neighbor; therefore love is the fulfillment of the law.

Rom. 13:10

Much more then, having now been justified by His blood, we shall be saved from wrath of God through Him.

Rom. 5:9 (NASB)

Now hope does not disappoint, because the love of God has been poured out in our hearts by the Holy Spirit who was given to us.

Rom. 5:5

Oh, the depth of the riches, both of the wisdom and knowledge of God! How unsearchable are His judgments and unfathomable His ways!

Rom. 11:33 (NASB)

Put on the Lord Jesus Christ, and make no provision for the flesh, to gratify its desires.

Rom. 13:14 (NRSV)

Q Yet in all these things we are more than *conquerors* through Him who loved us.

Rom. 8:37

Rejoice with those who rejoice, and weep with those who weep.

Rom. 12:15

So faith comes from hearing, and hearing by the word of Christ.

Rom. 10:17 (NASB)

There is therefore now no condemnation to those who are in Christ Jesus, who do not walk according to the flesh, but according to the Spirit.

Rom. 8:1

U For if we have become *united* with Him in the likeness of His death, certainly we shall also be in the likeness of His resurrection.

Rom. 6:5 (NASB)

V Do we then make *void* the law through faith? Certainly not! On the contrary, we establish the law.

Rom. 3:31

Whoever calls on the name of the Lord shall be saved.

Rom. 10:13

X For since the creation of the world, His invisible attributes, His eternal power and divine nature, have been clearly perceived, being understood by what has been made, so that they are without *excuse*.

Rom. 1:20 (NASB)

You are not in the flesh but in the Spirit, if indeed the Spirit of God dwells in you. Now if anyone does not have the Spirit of Christ, he is not His.

Rom. 8:9

Z As it is written: "Behold I lay in *Zion* a stumbling stone and rock of offense, and whoever believes on Him will not be put to shame."

Rom. 9:33

Writings of John

As the Father has loved Me, I have I loved you. Now remain in My love.

John 15:9 (NIV)

Behold what manner of love the Father has bestowed on us, that we should be called children of God! Therefore the world does not know us, because it did not know Him.

1 John 3:1

Come, see a man, which told me all things that ever I did: Is not this the Christ?

John 4:29 (KJV)

Do not love the world nor the things in the world. If anyone loves the world, the love of the Father is not in him.

1 John 2:15 (NASB)

Everyone who has this hope in him purifies himself, just as He is pure.

1 John 3:3

For God so loved the world that He gave His only begotten Son, that whoever believes in Him should not perish but have everlasting life.

John 3:16

God shall wipe away all tears from their eyes; and there shall be no more death, neither sorrow, nor crying, neither shall there be any more pain: for the former things are passed away.

Rev. 21:4 (KJV)

He who overcomes shall inherit all things, and I will be his God and He shall be My son.

Rev. 21:7

If we confess our sins, He is faithful and just to forgive us our sins, and to cleanse us from all unrighteousness.

1 John 1:9 (KJV)

Jesus said to him, "I am the way, and the truth, and the life. No one comes to the Father except through Me."

John 14:6 (NRSV)

K If we *know* that He hears us, whatever we ask, we *know* that we have the petitions that we have asked of Him.

1 John 5:15

Let not your heart be troubled; you believe in God, believe also in Me.

John 14:1

My little children, I am writing these things to you so that you may not sin. And if anyone sins, we have an Advocate with the Father, Jesus Christ the righteous.

1 John 2:1 (NASB)

No one can come to Me unless drawn by the Father who sent Me; and I will raise that person up on the last day.

John 6:44 (NRSV)

One of the elders said to me, "Do not weep. Behold, the Lion of the tribe of Judah, the Root of David, has prevailed to open the scroll and to loose its seven seals."

Rev. 5:5

Peace I leave with you; My peace I give to you. I do not give to you as the world gives. Do not let your hearts be troubled, and do not let them be afraid.

John 14:27 (NRSV)

Q And, behold, I come *quickly*; and My reward is with Me, to give every man according as his work shall be.

Rev. 22:12 (KJV)

Remember the word that I said to you, 'A servant is not greater than his master.' If they persecuted Me, they will also persecute you. If they kept My word, they will keep yours also.

John 15:20

S The *Spirit* and the bride say, "Come!" And let him who hears say, "Come!" And let him who thirsts come. Whoever desires, let him take the waters of life freely.

Rev. 22:17

There are three that bear record in heaven, the Father, the Word, and the Holy Ghost: and these three are one.

1 John 5:7 (KJV)

U Jesus answered and said to him, "Most assuredly, I say to you, *unless* one is born again, he cannot see the kingdom of God."

John 3:3

Verily, verily, I say unto thee, Except a man be born of water and of the Spirit, he cannot enter into the kingdom of God.

John 3:5 (KJV)

Whoever keeps His word, truly the love of God is perfected in him. By this we know that we are in Him.

1 John 2:5

X Just as the Father has life in Himself, so He has granted the Son also to have life in Himself; and He has given Him authority to *execute* judgment, because He is the Son of Man.

John 5:26, 27 (NRSV)

You are worthy, our Lord and God, to receive glory and honor and power, for You created all things, and by Your will they existed and were created.

Rev. 4:11 (NRSV)

Z As many as I love, I rebuke and chasten. Therefore be *zealous* and repent.

Rev. 3:19

Father, Son, and Holy Spirit

Characteristics of God

Awesome: "Come and see the works of God; He is *awesome* in His doing toward the sons of men."

Ps. 66:5

Benevolent: "Bless the Lord, O my soul, and forget not all His *benefits.*"

Ps. 103:2 (KJV)

Compassionate: "The Lord is gracious, and full of *compassion*; slow to anger, and of great mercy."

Ps. 145:8 (KJV)

Defender: "A father of the fatherless, a *defender* of widows, is God in His holy habitation."

Ps. 68:5

Eternal: "The *eternal* God is your refuge, and underneath are the everlasting arms."

Deut. 33:27a

Faithful: "Your *faithfulness* continues through all generations; You established the earth, and it endures."

Ps. 119:90 (NIV)

Gracious: "The Lord is merciful and *gracious,* slow to anger, and plenteous in mercy."

Ps. 103:8 (KJV)

Holy: "One cried to another and said: '*Holy, holy*, *holy* is the Lord of hosts; the whole earth is full of His glory!'"

Isa. 6:3

Immortal: "Now unto the King eternal, *immortal*, invisible, the only wise God, be honour and glory forever and ever. Amen."

1 Tim. 1:17 (KJV)

Just: "If we confess our sins, He is faithful and *just* to forgive us our sins, and to cleanse us from all unrighteousness."

1 John 1:9 (KJV)

Kind: "How precious is your *lovingkindness*, O God! Therefore the children of men put their trust under the shadow of your wings."

Ps. 36:7

Loving: "The Lord appeared to us in the past, saying: "I have *loved* you with an *everlasting love*; I have drawn you with unfailing kindness."

Jer. 31:3 (NIV)

Merciful: "As the heaven is high above the earth, so great is His *mercy* toward them that fear Him."

Ps. 103:11 (KJV)

Non-partial: "Then Peter opened his mouth and said: 'In truth I perceive that God shows *no partiality*.'"

Acts 10:34

Omniscient: "*Known* unto God are all His works from the beginning of the world."

Acts 15:18 (KJV)

Powerful: "God hath *power* to help, and to cast down."

2 Chron. 25:8b (KJV)

Quieting: "The work of righteousness will be peace, and the effect of righteousness, *quietness* and assurance forever."

Isa. 32:17

Righteous: "The Lord is *righteous*, He loves righteousness; His countenance beholds the upright."

Ps. 11:7

Steadfast: "He is a living God, and *steadfast* forever; His kingdom is the one that shall not be destroyed, and His kingdom shall endure to the end."

Dan. 6:26b

Trustworthy: "*Trust* in the Lord with all your heart, and lean not on your own understanding; in all your ways acknowledge Him, and he shall direct your paths."

Prov. 3:5, 6

Unchangeable: "**I** the Lord *do not change*. So you, the descendants of Jacob, are not destroyed."

Mal. 3:6 (NIV)

Valiant: "The right hand of the Lord is exalted; the right hand of the Lord does *valiantly*."

Ps. 118:16 (NASB)

Wise: "For the Lord gives *wisdom*; from His mouth come knowledge and understanding."

Prov. 2:6 (NASB)

X Excellent: "Sing to the Lord, for He has done *excellent* things; this is known in all the earth."

Isa. 12:5

Yahweh: "Behold, God *is* my salvation, I will trust and not be afraid; For *Yah*, the Lord, is my strength and song; He also has become my salvation."

Exod. 3:14

Zealous: "Thus says the Lord of hosts: 'I am *zealous* for Zion with great *zeal*; with great fervor I am *zealous* for her.'"

Zech. 8:2

God Is Able

As far as the east is from the west, so far has He removed our transgressions from us.

Ps. 103:12

Behold, I am the Lord, the God of all flesh; is anything too difficult for Me?

Jer. 32:27 (NASB)

Cast your burden on the Lord, and He will sustain you; He will never permit the righteous to be moved.

Ps. 55:22 (NRSV)

Delight yourself also in the Lord; and He will give you the desires of your heart.

Ps. 37:4 (NASB)

Even to your old age, I am He, and even to gray hairs I will carry you! I have made, and I will bear, even I will carry, and will deliver you.

Isa. 46:4

Fear not, for I am with you; be not dismayed, for I am your God. I will strengthen you, yes, I will help you, I will uphold you with My righteous right hand.

Isa. 41:10

God is our refuge and strength, an ever-present help in trouble.

Ps. 46:1 (NIV)

He delivers and rescues, He works signs and wonders in heaven and on earth; for He has saved Daniel from the power of the lions.

Dan. 6:27 (NRSV)

It shall come to pass that before they call, I will answer; and while they are still speaking, I will hear.

Isa. 65:24

Joseph named the firstborn Manasseh, "For," he said, "God has made me forget all my hardship and all my father's house."

Gen. 41:51 (NRSV)

K The Lord is your *keeper*; the Lord is your shade at your right hand.

Ps. 121:5 (NRSV)

Look to Me, and be saved, all you ends of the earth! For I am God, and there is no other.

Isa. 45:22

My God shall supply all your need according to His riches in glory by Christ Jesus.

Phil. 4:19 (KJV)

No weapon formed against you shall prosper, and every tongue which rises against you in judgment you shall condemn. This is the heritage of the servants of the Lord, and their righteousness is from Me," says the Lord.

Isa. 54:17

Our God is the God of salvation; and to God the Lord belong escapes from death.

Ps. 68:20

P I know whom I have believed and am *persuaded* that He is able to keep what I have committed to Him until that Day.

2 Tim. 1:12b

Q The Lord your God in your midst, the Mighty One, will save; He will rejoice over you with gladness, he will *quiet* you with His love, He will rejoice over you with singing.

Zeph. 3:17

Remember His marvelous works which He has done, His wonders, and the judgments of His mouth.

1 Chron. 16:12

Say to those with fearful hearts, "Be strong, do not fear; your God will come, He will come with vengeance; with divine retribution He will come to save you."

Isa. 35:4 (NIV)

Thus says the High and Lofty One who inhabits eternity, whose name is Holy: I dwell in the high and holy place, and also with those who are contrite and humble in spirit, to revive the spirit of the humble, and to revive the heart of the contrite.

Isa. 57:15 (NRSV)

Unless the Lord builds the house, they labor in vain who build it; unless the Lord guards the city, the watchman stays awake in vain.

Ps. 127:1

Verily, verily, I say unto you, The hour is coming, and now is, when the dead shall hear the voice of the Son of God; and they that hear shall live.

John 5:25 (KJV)

With man this is impossible, but with God all things are possible.

Matt. 19:26b (NIV)

X As for the Almighty, we cannot find him; He is *excellent* in power, in judgment and abundant justice; He does not oppress.

Job 37:23

You know when I sit down and when I rise up; You discern my thoughts from far away.

Ps. 139:2 (NRSV)

Z Do not be afraid **Zion**.... The Lord your God is in your midst, a victorious warrior. He will rejoice over you with joy, He will be quiet in His love, He will rejoice over you with shouts of joy.

Zeph. 3:16, 17 (NASB)

His Word

As newborn babes, desire the pure milk of the word, that you may grow thereby, if indeed you have tasted that the Lord is gracious.

1 Peter 2:2, 3

Be doers of the word, and not merely hearers, who deceive themselves.

James 1:22 (NRSV)

Continue earnestly in prayer, being vigilant in it with thanksgiving; meanwhile praying also for us, that God would open to us a door for the word, to speak the mystery of Christ, for which I am also in chains.

Col. 4:2, 3

Do not add to His words, or else He will rebuke you, and you will be found a liar.

Prov. 30:6 (NRSV)

Every word of God is pure: He is a shield unto them that put their trust in Him.

Prov. 30:5 (KJV)

Forever, Lord, Your word stands in heaven.

Ps. 119:89 (NASB)

Grass withers, the flower fades; but the word of our God will stand forever.

Isa. 40:8 (NRSV)

He humbled you by letting you hunger, then by feeding you with manna, with which neither you nor your ancestors were acquainted, in order to make you understand that one does not live by bread alone, but by every word that comes from the mouth of the Lord.

Deut. 8:3 (NRSV)

I rejoice at Your word as one who finds great treasure.

Ps. 119:162

J The entirety of Your word is truth, and every one of Your righteous *judgments* endures forever.

Ps. 119:160

K I *know* your works. See, I have set before you an open door, and no one can shut it; for you have a little strength, have *kep*t My word, and have not denied My name.

Rev. 3:8

Let the word of Christ richly dwell within you, with all wisdom teaching and admonishing one another with psalms, hymns, and spiritual songs, singing with thankfulness in your hearts to God.

Col. 3:16 (NASB)

My soul faints for Your salvation, but I hope in Your word.

Ps. 119:81

Now this is the parable: the seed is the word of God.

Luke 8:11 (NASB)

Ones that fell on the good ground are those who, having heard the word with a noble and good heart, keep it and bear fruit with patience.

Luke 8:15

Paul and Barnabas grew bold and said, "It was necessary that the word of God should be spoken to you first; but since you reject it, and judge yourselves unworthy of everlasting life, behold, we turn to the Gentiles."

Acts 13:46

Q A bishop, as God's steward, must be blameless; he must not be arrogant or *quick-tempered* or addicted to wine or violent or greedy for gain; but he must be hospitable, a lover of goodness, prudent, upright, devout, and self-controlled. He must have a firm grasp of the word that is trustworthy in accordance with the teaching, so that he may be able both to preach with sound doctrine and to refute those who contradict it.

Titus 1:7–9 (NRSV)

Remember Your word to Your servant, in which you have made me hope. This is my comfort in my distress, that Your promise gives me life.

Ps. 119:49, 50 (NRSV)

Sanctify them by the truth; Your word is truth.

John 17:17 (NIV)

Take the helmet of salvation, and the sword of the Spirit, which is the word of God.

Eph. 6:17

Uphold me according to Your word, that I may live; and do not let me be ashamed of my hope.

Ps. 119:116

Very truly, I tell you, anyone who hears My word, and believes Him who sent Me has eternal life, and does not come under judgment, but has passed from death to life.

John 5:24 (NRSV)

Whoever follows His word, in him the love of God has truly been perfected. By this we know that we are in Him.

1 John 2:5 (NASB)

X Bless the Lord, you His angels, who *excel* in strength, who do His word, heeding the voice of His word.

Ps. 103:20

Your word is a lamp to my feet and a light to my path.

Ps. 119:105 ([NASB)

Z My *zeal* has consumed me, because my enemies have forgotten Your words.

Ps. 119:139 (NASB)

Kingdom of God

Again, the kingdom of heaven is like treasure hidden in a field, which a man found and hid; and for joy over it he goes and sells all that he has and buys that field.

Matt. 13:44

But seek first the kingdom of God and His righteousness, and all these things shall be added to you.

Matt. 6:33

Come, you who are blessed of My Father, inherit the kingdom prepared for you from the foundation of the world.

Matt. 25:34b (NASB)

Do you not know that wrongdoers will not inherit the kingdom of God?

1 Cor. 6:9a (NRSV)

E In this way, *entry* into the *eternal* kingdom of our Lord and Savior Jesus Christ will be richly provided for you.

2 Pet. 1:11 (NRSV)

For He is the living God, and steadfast forever; His kingdom is the one which shall not be destroyed, and His dominion shall endure to the end.

Dan. 6:26b

God is my King from of old, working salvation in the midst of the earth.

Ps. 74:12

His dominion is an everlasting dominion, and His kingdom is from generation to generation.

Dan. 4:34b

In the days of those kings the God of heaven will set up a kingdom which will never be destroyed, and that kingdom will not be left for another people; it will crush and put an end to all these kingdoms, but it will itself endure forever.

Dan. 2:44 (NASB)

Jesus said to him, "No one, after putting his hand to the plow and looking back, is fit for the kingdom of God."

Luke 9:62 (NASB)

K "The *kingdoms* of this world have become the *kingdoms* of our Lord and of His Christ, and He shall reign forever and ever!"

Rev. 11:15b

L The *Lord* has established His throne in heaven, and His kingdom rules over all.

Ps. 103:19 (NIV)

My kingdom is not of this world. If My kingdom were of this world, My servants would be fighting so that I would not be handed over to the Jews; but as it is, My kingdom is not of this realm.

John 18:36 (NASB)

Now when Jesus saw that he answered wisely, He said to him, "You are not far from the kingdom of God."

Mark 12:34a

Oh, clap your hands, all you peoples! Shout to God with the voice of triumph! For the Lord Most High is awesome; He is a great King over all the earth.

Ps. 47:1, 2

Pilate therefore said to Him, "Are You a king then?" Jesus answered, "You say rightly that I am a king. For this cause I was born, and for this cause I have come into the world, that I should bear witness to the truth. Everyone who is of the truth hears My voice."

John 18:37

Q My people will abide in a peaceful habitation, in secure dwellings, and in *quiet* resting places.

Isa. 32:18 (NRSV)

Repent, for the kingdom of heaven is at hand.

Matt. 3:2 (NASB)

Since we are receiving a kingdom which cannot be shaken, let us be thankful, and so worship God acceptably with reverence and awe.

Heb. 12:28 (NIV)

Then comes the end, when He hands over the kingdom to our God and Father, when He has abolished all rule and all authority and power.

1 Cor. 15:24 (NASB)

Until the Ancient of Days came, and judgment was made in favor of the saints of the Most High, and the time came for the saints to possess the kingdom.

Dan. 7:22

Verily, verily, I say unto thee, Except a man be born again, he cannot see the kingdom of God.

John 3:3b (KJV)

When the Son of Man comes in His glory, and all the angels with Him, then He will sit on the throne of His glory.

Matt. 25:31 (NRSV)

X Yours, O Lord are the greatness, the power, the glory, the victory, and the majesty; for all that is in the heavens and on the earth is Yours; Yours is the kingdom, O Lord, and You are *exalted* as head above all.

1 Chron. 29:11 (NRSV)

Your throne, O God, is forever and ever; a scepter of righteousness is the scepter of Your kingdom.

Ps. 45:6

Z "I have installed My King on *Zion*, My holy mountain."

Ps. 2:6 (NIV)

Names and Descriptions of Jesus Christ

Advocate: "My little children, these things I write to you, so that you may not sin. And if anyone sins, we have an *Advocate* with the Father, Jesus Christ the righteous."

1 John 2:1

Bread of Life: "Jesus said to them, 'I am the *bread of life*; the one who comes to Me will not be hungry, and the one who believes in Me will never be thirsty.'"

John 6:35 (NASB)

Chief Cornerstone: "Therefore it is also contained in the scripture, 'Behold, I lay in Zion a *chief cornerstone*, elect, precious, and he who believes on Him will by no means be put to shame.'"

1 Peter 2:6

Deliverer: "And so all Israel will be saved; just as it is written, 'The *Deliverer* will come from Zion. He will remove ungodliness from Jacob.'"

Rom. 11:26 (NASB)

Emmanuel: "Behold, a virgin shall be with child, and shall bring forth a son, and they shall call His name *Emmanuel,* which being interpreted is, God with us."

Matt. 1:23 (KJV)

Friend: "The Son of Man has come eating and drinking, and you say, 'Look, a glutton and a drunkard, a *friend* of tax collectors and sinners!'"

Luke 7:34 (NRSV)

God: "Then He said to Thomas, 'Reach your finger here, and look at My hands; and reach your hand here, and put it into My side. Do not be unbelieving, but believing.' And Thomas answered and said to Him, 'My Lord and my *God*!'"

John 20:27, 28

Holy One: "You denied the *Holy One* and the Just, and asked for a murderer to be granted to you."

Acts 3:14

I Am: "Jesus said to them, 'Truly, truly I say to you, before Abraham was born, *I am*.'"

John 8:58 (NASB)

Judge: "He commanded us to preach to the people, and to testify that it is He who was ordained by God to be Judge of the living and the dead."

Acts 10:42

King of Kings: "He has on His robe and on His thigh a name written: *King of Kings* and Lord of Lords."

Rev. 19:16

Lamb: "The next day John saw Jesus coming toward him, and said, 'Behold! The *Lamb* of God who takes away the sin of the world!'"

John 1:29

Messiah: "The first thing Andrew did was to find his brother Simon and tell him, 'We have found the *Messiah*' (that is, the Christ)."

John 1:41 (NIV)

Nazarene: "He went and lived in a town called Nazareth. So was fulfilled what was said through the prophets, that He would be called a *Nazarene*."

Matt. 2:23 (NIV)

Omega: "I am the Alpha and the *Omega,* the Beginning and the End, the First and the Last."

Rev. 22:13

Prince of Peace: "For unto us a Child is born, unto us a Son is given; and the government will be upon His shoulder. And His name will be called Wonderful, Counselor, Mighty God, Everlasting Father, *Prince of Peace*."

Isa. 9:6

Quickening Spirit: "And so it is written, the first man Adam was made a living soul; the last Adam was made a *quickening spirit*."

1 Cor. 15:45 (KJV)

Redeemer: "'A *Redeemer* will come to Zion, and to those who turn from wrongdoing,' declares the Lord."

Isa. 59:20 (NASB)

Saviour: "For unto you is born this day in the city of David a *Saviour*, which is Christ the Lord."

Luke 2:11 (KJV)

Truth: "Jesus said to him, 'I am the way, the *truth*, and the life. No one comes to the Father except through Me.'"

John 14:6

Unspeakable Gift: "Thanks be unto God for His *unspeakable gift*."

2 Cor. 9:15 (KJV)

Vine: "I am the *vine*, you are the branches. He who abides in Me, and I in him, bears much fruit; for without Me you can do nothing."

John 15:5

Word: "In the beginning was the *Word*, and the *Word* was with God, and the *Word* was God."

John 1:1 (KJV)

Xristos: "Therefore, when they had gathered together, Pilate said to them, 'Whom do you want me to release to you? Barabbas, or Jesus who is called *Christ?*'"
(Christ is translated from the Greek word, Xristos, meaning Anointed or Messiah)

Matt. 27:17

Young Child: "And when they had come into the house, they saw the *young Child* with Mary His mother, and fell down and worshiped Him. And when they had opened their treasures, they presented gifts to Him: gold, frankincense, and myrrh."

Matt. 2:11

Zeal for Your House: "He said to those who sold doves, 'Take these things away! Do not make My Father's house a house of merchandise!' Then His disciples remembered that it is written, '*Zeal for Your house* has eaten Me up.'"

John 2:16, 17

Second Coming of Christ

As the lightning comes from the east and flashes to the west, so also will the coming of the Son of Man be.

Matt. 24:27

Behold, I am coming quickly! Hold fast what you have, that no one take your crown.

Rev. 3:11

Christ was sacrificed once to take away the sins of many; and He will appear a second time, not to bear sin, but to bring salvation to those who are waiting for Him.

Heb. 9:28 (NIV)

Do not be astonished at this; for the hour is coming when all who are in their graves will hear His voice and will come out—those who have done good, to the resurrection of life, and those who have done evil, to the resurrection of condemnation.

John 5:28, 29 (NRSV)

Every eye shall see Him, and they also which pierced Him: and all kindreds of the earth shall wail because of Him. Even so, Amen.

Rev. 1:7b (KJV)

Finally, there is laid up for me the crown of righteousness, which the Lord, the righteous Judge, will give to me on that Day, and not to me only but also to all who have loved His appearing.

2 Tim. 4:8

Go, therefore, and make disciples of all the nations, baptizing them in the name of the Father and the Son and the Holy Spirit, teaching them to follow all that I commanded you; and behold, I am with you always, to the end of the age.

Matt. 28:19, 20 (NASB)

He shall send His angels with a great sound of a trumpet, and they shall gather together His elect from the four winds, from one end of heaven to the other.

Matt. 24:31 (KJV)

I charge you therefore before God and the Lord Jesus Christ, who will judge the living and the dead at His appearing and His kingdom: Preach the word! Be ready in season and out of season.

2 Tim 4:1, 2a

Jesus knew that they wanted to ask Him, so He said to them, "Are you discussing among yourselves what I meant when I said, 'A little while, and you will no longer see Me, and again a little while, and you will see Me?'

John 16:19 (NRSV)

Know this, that if the master of the house had known what hour the thief would come, he would have watched and not allowed his house to be broken into. Therefore you also be ready, for the Son of Man is coming at an hour you do not expect.

Matt. 24:43, 44

L The *Lord* Himself shall descend from heaven with a shout, with the voice of the archangel, and with the trump of God: and the dead in Christ shall rise first.

1 Thess. 4:16 (KJV)

Men of Galilee," they said, "why do you stand here looking into the sky? This same Jesus, who has been taken from you into heaven, will come back in the same way you have seen Him go into heaven."

Acts 1:11 (NIV)

Now may the God of peace Himself sanctify you completely; and may your whole spirit, soul, and body be preserved blameless at the coming of our Lord Jesus Christ.

1 Thess. 5:23

Of that day and hour no one knows, not even the angels of heaven, but My Father only.

Matt 24:36

P If I go and *prepare* a *place* for you, I am coming again and will take you to Myself, so that where I am, there you also will be.

John 14:3 (NASB)

Q Behold, I am coming *quickly*, and My reward is with Me, to reward each one as his work deserves.

Rev. 22:12 (NASB)

Remember Lot's wife. "In that day, he who is on the housetop, and his goods are in the house, let him not come down to take them away. And likewise the one who is in the field, let him not turn back."

Luke 17:32, 31

Surely, I come quickly. Amen. Even so, come, Lord Jesus.

Rev. 22:20b (KJV)

Then the sign of the Son of Man will appear in heaven, and then all the tribes of the earth will mourn, and they will see the Son of Man coming on the clouds of heaven with power and great glory.

Matt. 24:30

Unless you repent you will all likewise perish.

Luke 13:3b

Verily, verily, I say unto you, The hour is coming, and now is, when the dead shall hear the voice of the Son of God: and they that hear shall live.

John 5:25 (KJV)

Watch therefore, for you do not know what hour your Lord is coming.

Matt. 24:42

X Exhort one another daily, while it is called "Today," lest any of you be hardened through the deceitfulness of sin. For we have become partakers of Christ if we hold the beginning of our confidence steadfast to the end.

Heb. 3:13, 14

You yourselves know perfectly that the day of the Lord so comes as a thief in the night.

1 Thess. 5:2

Z Indeed the Lord has proclaimed to the end of the world: "Say to the daughter of *Zion*, 'Surely your salvation is coming; behold, His reward is with Him, and His work before Him.'"

Isa. 62:11

Words of Christ

Ask, and it will be given to you; seek, and you will find; knock, and it will be opened to you.

Matt. 7:7

Blessed are the poor in spirit: for theirs is the kingdom of heaven.

Matt. 5:3 (KJV)

Come to Me, all who are weary and burdened, and I will give you rest.

Matt. 11:28 (NASB)

Do not think that I came to destroy the Law or the Prophets. I did not come to destroy but to fulfill.

Matt. 5:17

Enter through the narrow gate; for the gate is wide and the way is broad that leads to destruction, and there are many who enter through it.

Matt. 7:13 (NASB)

Follow Me, and I will make you fishers of men.

Matt. 4:19b

Go therefore and make disciples of all nations, baptizing them in the name of the Father and of the Son and of the Holy Spirit.

Matt. 28:19 (NRSV)

Heaven and earth shall pass away: but My words shall not pass away.

Luke 21:33 (KJV)

I am the way, and the truth, and the life. No one comes to the Father except through Me.

John 14:6b (NRSV)

Judge not, that you be not judged.

Matt. 7:1

K The *kingdom* of heaven is like treasure hidden in a field. When a man found it, he hid it again, and then in his joy went and sold all that he had and bought that field.

Matt. 13:44 (NIV)

Love your enemies, bless them that curse you, do good to them that hate you, and pray for them which despitefully use you, and persecute you.

Matt. 5:44b (KJV)

Most assuredly, I say to you, unless a grain of wheat falls into the ground and dies, it remains alone; but if it dies, it produces much grain.

John 12:24

Not everyone who says to Me, 'Lord, Lord,' shall enter the kingdom of heaven, but he who does the will of My Father in heaven.

Matt. 7:21

Other sheep I have, which are not of this fold: them also I must bring, and they shall hear My voice; and there shall be one fold, and one shepherd.

John 10:16 (KJV)

Peace I leave with you, My peace I give to you; not as the world gives do I give to you. Let not your heart be troubled, neither let it be afraid.

John 14:27

Q The *Queen* of the South will rise up with this generation at the judgment and will condemn it, because she came from the ends of the earth to hear the wisdom of Solomon; and behold, something greater than Solomon is here.

Matt. 12:42 (NASB)

Render therefore to Caesar the things that are Caesar's, and to God the things that are God's.

Luke 20:25b

Seek first the kingdom of God and His righteousness, and all these things shall be added to you.

Matt. 6:33

This is My commandment, that you love one another, just as I have loved you.

John 15:12 (NASB)

Unless your righteousness exceeds the righteousness of the scribes and Pharisees, you will by no means enter the kingdom of heaven.

Matt. 5:20b

Verily, verily, I say unto thee, except a man be born of water and of the Spirit, he cannot enter into the kingdom of God.

John 3:5b (KJV)

Whatever you want men to do to you, do also to them, for this is the Law and the Prophets.

Matt. 7:12

X Whoever *exalts* himself shall be humbled, and whoever humbles himself shall be *exalted*.

Matt. 23:12 (NASB)

You are the light of the world. A city that is set on a hill cannot be hidden.

Matt. 5:14

Zacchaeus, make haste and come down, for today I must stay at your house.

Luke 19:5b

The Holy Spirit

As I began to speak, the Holy Spirit fell upon them, as upon us at the beginning. Then I remembered the word of the Lord, how He said, 'John indeed baptized with water, but you shall be baptized with the Holy Spirit.'

Acts 11:15, 16

By one Spirit we were all baptized into one body, whether Jews or Greeks, whether slaves or free, and we were all made to drink of one Spirit.

1 Cor. 12:13 (NASB)

Come near to Me, hear this: I have not spoken in secret from the beginning; from the time that it was, I *was* there. And now the Lord God and His Spirit have sent Me.

Isa. 48:16

Daniel came before me (his name *is* Belteshazzar, according to the name of my god; in him is the Spirit of the Holy God), and I told the dream before him.

Dan. 4:8b

E The *earth* was without form, and void; and darkness was upon the face of the deep. And the Spirit of God moved upon the face of the waters.

Gen. 1:2 (KJV)

For there are three that bear witness in heaven: the Father, the Word, and the Holy Spirit; and these three are one.

1 John 5:7

God has revealed them to us through His Spirit. For the Spirit searches all things, yes, the deep things of God.

1 Cor. 2:10

However, when He, the Spirit of truth, has come, He will guide you into all truth; for He will not speak on His own authority, but whatever He hears He will speak; and He will tell you things to come.

John 16:13

If you then, though you are evil, know how to give good gifts to your children, how much more will your Father in heaven give the Holy Spirit to those who ask Him!

Luke 11:13 (NRSV)

Jesus was led up by the Spirit into the wilderness to be tempted by the devil.

Matt. 4:1

K The *kingdom* of God is not eating and drinking, but righteousness and peace and joy in the Holy Spirit.

Rom. 14:17 (NASB)

L The *Lord* said to Moses, "Take Joshua the son of Nun, a man in whom is the Spirit, and lay your hand on him."

Num. 27:18 (NASB)

M But the *manifestation* of the Spirit is given to each one for the profit of all.

1 Cor. 12:7

Now when the apostles at Jerusalem heard that Samaria had accepted the word of God, they sent Peter and John to them. The two went down and prayed for them that they might receive the Holy Spirit.

Acts 8:14, 15 (NRSV)

One and the same Spirit works all these things, distributing to each one individually just as He wills.

1 Cor. 12:11 (NASB)

Prophecy never came by the will of man, but holy men of God spoke *as they were* moved by the Holy Spirit.

2 Peter 1:21

Q The *queen* spoke, saying, "O king, live forever! Do not let your thoughts trouble you, nor let your countenance change. There is a man in your kingdom in whom *is* the Spirit of the Holy God."

Dan. 5:10b, 11a

R Then His people *remembered* the days of old, of Moses. Where is He who brought them up out of the sea with the shepherds of His flock? Where is He who put His Holy Spirit in the midst of them?

Isa. 63:11 (NASB)

S The *Spirit* of the Lord God is upon me, because the Lord anointed me to bring good news to the humble; He has sent me to bind up the brokenhearted, to proclaim release to captives and freedom to prisoners.

Isa. 61:1 (NASB)

They were all filled with the Holy Spirit and began to speak with other tongues, as the Spirit gave them utterance.

Acts 2:4

U Make every effort to keep the *unity* of the Spirit through the bond of peace.

Eph. 4:3 (NIV)

V Or do you think that the Scripture says in *vain*, "The Spirit who dwells in us yearns jealously"?

James 4:5

When Jesus had been baptized, just as he came up from the water, suddenly the heavens were opened to him and he saw the Spirit of God descending like a dove and alighting on him.

Matt. 3:16 (NRSV)

X Now the Spirit *expressly* says that in later times some will renounce the faith by paying attention to deceitful spirits and teachings of demons.

1 Tim. 4:1 (NRSV)

You, beloved, building yourselves up on your most holy faith, praying in the Holy Spirit, keep yourselves in the love of God, looking for the mercy of our Lord Jesus Christ unto eternal life.

Jude 1:20, 21

Z Then Moses said to him, "Are you *zealous* for my sake? Oh, that all the Lord's people were prophets and that the Lord would put His Spirit upon them!"

Num. 11:29

What's Next?

You might be asking, "What else can I do with these A–Z Bible verses?" Here are some suggestions:

- Select an encouraging verse to write in a birthday, encouragement, get well or sympathy card.
- Choose verses to commit to memory that will bring comfort to yourself in troubling times.
- Study the themes of the Bible to get a greater understanding of them.
- Give further study to the verses that you don't quite understand.
- Read the entire chapter associated with each verse so as to understand its context.
- Use the texts to give a Bible study or prepare a sermon.
- Create an acrostic of the name of a family member or friend as a special gift. Present it in a lovely frame. See the face of the recipient glow! For example:

Rest in the Lord ... Ps. 37:7
Unto the upright ... Ps. 112:4
Blessed is he ... Ps. 32:1
You shall call ... Isa. 58:9

TEACH Services, Inc.
P U B L I S H I N G

We invite you to view the complete
selection of titles we publish at:
www.TEACHServices.com

We encourage you to write us
with your thoughts about this,
or any other book we publish at:
info@TEACHServices.com

TEACH Services' titles may be purchased in
bulk quantities for educational, fund-raising,
business, or promotional use.
bulksales@TEACHServices.com

Finally, if you are interested in seeing
your own book in print, please contact us at:
publishing@TEACHServices.com
We are happy to review your manuscript at no charge.